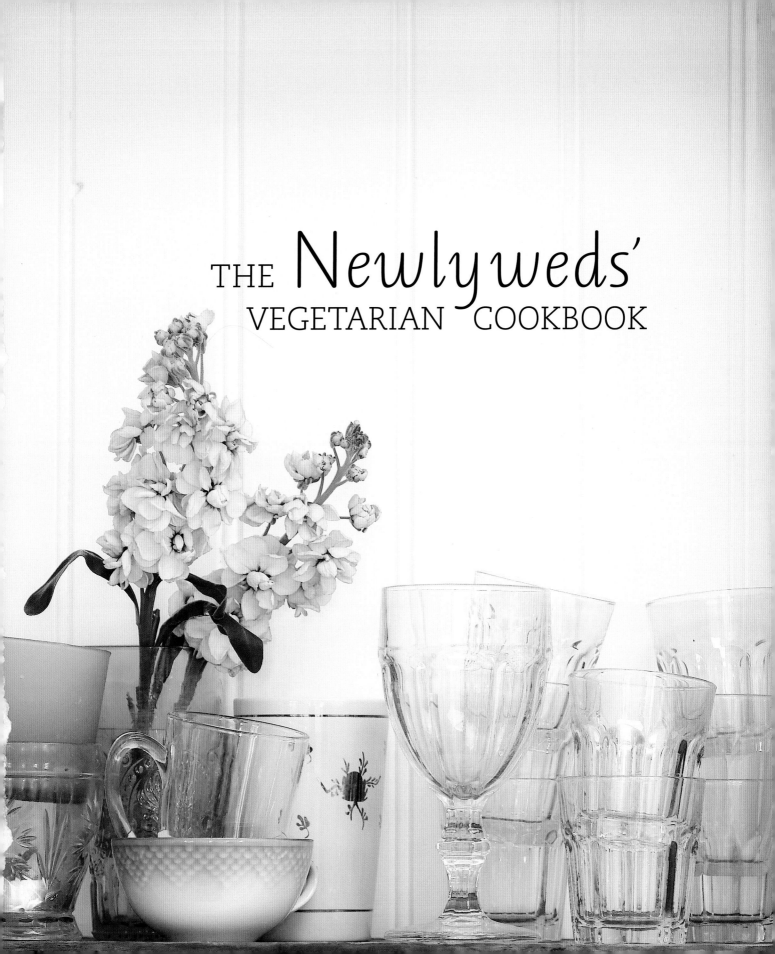

THE Newlyweds'
VEGETARIAN COOKBOOK

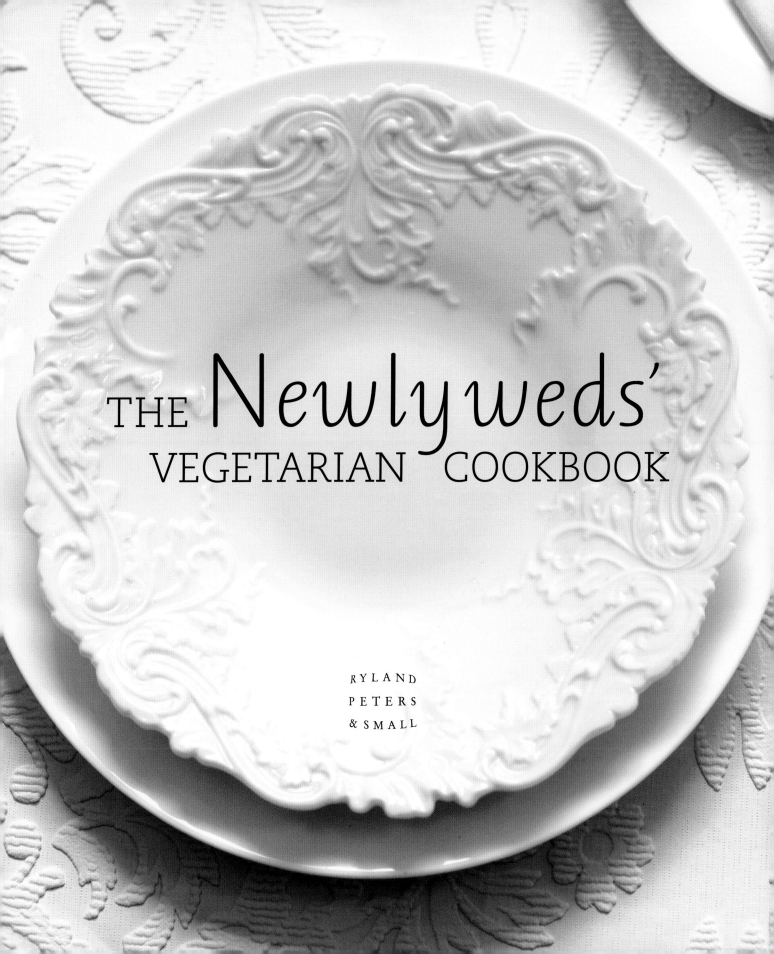

THE Newlyweds'
VEGETARIAN COOKBOOK

RYLAND
PETERS
& SMALL

Senior Designer Iona Hoyle
Editor Rebecca Woods
Picture Research Emily Westlake
Production Maria Petalidou
Art Director Leslie Harrington
Publishing Director Alison Starling
Indexer Hilary Bird

First published in 2011
by Ryland Peters & Small
20–21 Jockey's Fields
London WC1R 4BW
and
Ryland Peters & Small, Inc.
519 Broadway, 5th Floor
New York, NY 10012

www.rylandpeters.com

10 9 8 7 6 5 4 3 2 1

ISBN 978 1 84975 115 5

A CIP record for this book is available
from the British Library.

[US CIP data has been applied for]

Printed in China

For digital editions visit
www.rylandpeters.com/apps.php

Notes

• All spoon measurements are level
unless otherwise specified.

• Eggs are medium unless otherwise
specified. Uncooked or partly cooked eggs
should not be served to the very young,
the very old, those with compromised
immune systems, or to pregnant women.

• Weights and measurements have been
rounded up or down slightly to make
measuring easier.

• Ovens should be preheated to the
specified temperature. If using a
fan-assisted oven, cooking times should
be reduced according to the
manufacturer's instructions.

• To sterilize preserving jars, wash them
in hot, soapy water and rinse in boiling
water. Place in a large saucepan and cover
with hot water. With the saucepan lid on,
bring the water to a boil and continue
boiling for 15 minutes. Turn off the heat
and leave the jars in the hot water until
just before they are to be filled. Invert the
jars onto a clean dish towel to dry.
Sterilize the lids for 5 minutes, by boiling
or according to the manufacturer's
instructions. Jars should be filled and
sealed while they are still hot.

contents

introduction

Getting married is one of the most exciting moments of your life. After the joys of the day itself, there are the delights of setting up home together. One of the many pleasures of married life is cooking for your loved one or, better still, preparing a meal together. You will no doubt receive a range of wonderful wedding gifts for your new home, and for the first time in your lives you might have a well-equipped kitchen or a full dinner service, which is sure to inspire you to cook up some delicious meals for your partner, family, and friends.

This is where *The Newlyweds' Vegetarian Cookbook* comes into its own. Whether you are new to vegetarian cooking or a seasoned cook, it is a delicious source of culinary inspiration for every day of your new married life together. First, Kitchen Basics talks you through all the essential equipment and food items you will need in order to put a meal together. Then the recipe chapters cover everything from Brunch to Family Gatherings and Drinks. From quick weekday dinners that can be thrown together at the end of a busy day, to Special Occasions when you want to push the boat out and make something really memorable, this book is packed with dozens of exciting ideas for meat-free dishes. And because all the recipes are so easy-to-follow, you'll never be afraid to try something new.

The Newlyweds' Vegetarian Cookbook is comprehensive and inspiring. It will become an invaluable cooking partner during your new married life and many of the recipes are destined to become family favorites in the years ahead. It is a book that will make cooking for your loved one, family, and friends a true pleasure, whatever the occasion.

kitchen basics

Before you even begin cooking, there is essential equipment you will need to make your kitchen function as it should. You will find this listed on page 11. It is also a good idea to ensure your storecupboard is stocked with basic cooking ingredients so you always have them to hand when necessary. Keeping a well-stocked pantry will mean you can put together a meal in minutes on those really hectic days when you have no time to go shopping.

utensils, pots, & pans

Whether you are a new cook or experienced in the kitchen, this list of essential equipment is what you will need to put the most basic of meals on the table. You may already have a number of these items, or received some of them as wedding gifts, so take all the equipment you already have out of the cupboards and drawers and lay it on the table. Check the list, opposite, to see if you have everything you need, then put it back in its place. If there's any equipment left on the table that you haven't used in the last 12 months, give it away. As funds allow, try to assemble all the equipment in the startup kit. Perhaps your friends and family can be persuaded to give you the items on the wish list for Christmas and birthdays.

Startup kit

For a basic set of equipment, buy the best
you can afford, then it will last.

In your cupboards

1 non-stick skillet/frying pan

1 non-stick wok with lid

1 heavy shallow pan with
ovenproof handles for stove-top
or oven cooking

3 saucepans—small, medium,
and very large—with lids

1 collapsible metal steamer,
bamboo steamer, or 2-tier
steaming saucepan

1 wire cooling rack

1 hand-held blender

1 strainer/sieve

1 colander with legs or stand

1 box grater

1 set of mixing bowls

1 set of measuring cups

1 measuring pitcher/jug

1 lemon juicer

1 salad spinner

On the shelf

1 set of kitchen scales

salt and pepper mills

1 cafetière and/or 1 teapot

In a block or wrap

1 paring or utility knife

1 large chopping knife

1 bread knife

1 pair of kitchen scissors

1 sharpening steel

On the work surface

1 heavy wooden chopping board

1 roll of paper kitchen towels

In a large utensil pot

2 wooden spoons

1 large metal spoon

1 large slotted metal spoon

1 ladle

1 potato masher

1 long handled spatula

2 plastic spatulas

1 set of salad servers

1 pair of tongs

In the top drawer

1 potato peeler

1 can opener

1 corkscrew

2 metal skewers

1 rolling pin

In the bottom drawer

wax/greaseproof paper

aluminum foil

plastic wrap/cling film

medium freezer bags

large heavy-duty
trash bags

kitchen string

dish towels/tea towels

apron

oven mitts/gloves

For the oven

1 non-stick roasting pan

1 non-stick baking sheet

12-hole non-stick muffin pan

2 round cake pans
(8 inch/20 cm diameter)

Wish list

Put these desirable objects on your
"wish list" for Christmas and birthdays.

In your cupboards

1 food processor

1 electric mixer

1 blender

1 stove-top grill/griddle pan

6 ramekins (⅔ cup/150 ml)

3 glass bowls—small, medium
and large

1 cooking thermometer

1 olive oil drizzler

1 mortar and pestle

In a large utensil pot

1 metal whisk

1 palette knife

1 meshed spoon for
deep-frying

In the top drawer

parchment paper

large freezer bags

1 pastry brush

In the bottom drawer

more dish towels/tea towels
(12 total)

another apron

another set of oven
mitts/gloves

For the oven

another non-stick roasting pan

another non-stick baking
sheet

1 loose-bottomed flan ring
(10 inch/25 cm diameter)

1 non-stick springform cake
pan (8 inch/20 cm diameter)

1 cake pan (7 inch/18 cm
square)

pantry
essentials

It is a good idea to keep your pantry well stocked with useful ingredients that can be thrown together at a moment's notice to produce a quick meal. These are the essentials that are listed on the right. Fresh food should be bought often and in small quantities so it is always the freshest it can be. The food listed is just an illustration of the sorts of things you might want on hand at any one time.

Essentials

Staples

2–3 packages pasta, various shapes

2–3 packages rice—long grain, basmati, Thai fragrant, risotto

egg or rice noodles

dried lentils

all-purpose/plain and self-rising flour

baking powder

coffee, tea, and sugar

Cans and cartons

vegetable bouillon (broth)

cans of: chopped tomatoes, chickpeas, cannellini beans, and borlotti beans

coconut cream or milk

Oils and vinegars

large bottles of olive oil and safflower/sunflower oil

small bottles of extra virgin olive oil for salads, peanut oil for frying, chile oil for flavoring

balsamic vinegar

red and white wine vinegar

Spices

whole nutmeg

ground cumin

ground coriander

ground turmeric

ground cinnamon and cinnamon sticks

sweet paprika

dried hot pepper flakes/dried chilli flakes

Seasonings and flavorings

coarse sea salt

black peppercorns

soy sauce (light and dark)

Tabasco sauce

teriyaki sauce

smooth Dijon mustard

clear honey

vanilla extract

Fresh food

a bag of onions

a head of garlic

red chiles

fresh root ginger

fresh herbs, such as parsley

carrots

potatoes

tomatoes

lemons, limes, oranges, apples, and pears

In the refrigerator

eggs

milk

unsalted butter

a wedge of Parmesan cheese

feta cheese

Greek or plain yogurt

In the freezer

vanilla ice cream

frozen peas

ice cubes

Extra items

When you've got the basics, begin adding these extra ingredients for more adventurous cooking.

Staples

couscous or cracked wheat

bread flour

dry yeast

old-fashioned rolled oats

sultanas (golden raisins) or raisins

cocoa powder

superfine/caster sugar

brown sugar

Oils and vinegars

small bottles of sesame oil and walnut oil

Spices

saffron threads

Seasonings and flavorings

horseradish sauce

whole-grain mustard

English mustard powder

sun-dried tomatoes and peppers

black olives

caperberries/capers

red wine

brandy

Marsala or sherry

Fresh food

your choice of other herbs, such as chives, basil, thyme, and rosemary

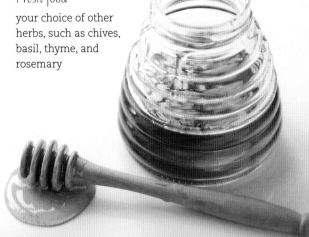

china, glassware, & flatware

Now that you are married, you may be entertaining family and friends more frequently than you did previously. Even when just the two of you are eating together, it's important to make mealtimes special from time to time, especially at the end of a long week or when you are celebrating a special occasion. Using your best table- and glassware can make even the simplest food look amazing. You may have received a number of the items listed opposite as wedding gifts, or own them already, but here is a list of the glassware and tableware you may need to entertain a group of eight for dinner (depending on what dishes and drinks are being served).

China
8 dinner plates

8 side plates

8 soup bowls

8 dessert plates or dishes

8 cups and saucers

Flatware/cutlery
8 dinner forks

8 salad forks

8 dinner knives

8 butter knives

8 soup spoons

8 dessert spoons and/or forks

8 teaspoons

Serving pieces
2 ladles—1 large and 1 small

sugar spoon or tongs

salad servers

1 large, three-pronged fork

2–3 serving spoons

pie server

Serving dishes
2 platters—1 large and 1 small

serving bowls—3 sizes

sauce or gravy boat

water pitcher/jug

cream pitcher/jug

sugar bowl

teapot and/or coffee pot

variety of small dishes

Glassware
8 water glasses

8 red wine glasses

8 white wine glasses

8 juice glasses

8 highball glasses

8 champagne flutes

8 brandy glasses

8 martini glasses

8 margarita glasses

8 liqueur glasses

Tableware
tablecloth

8 napkins

heatproof mats

brunch

Two superb pancake recipes to start the day: the Orange Cornmeal Hotcakes have a citrusy tang to them, and a slightly granular crunch from the cornmeal. Perfect Blueberry Pancakes should be light and fluffy, with a good rise on them. The secret is to use some water—an all-milk batter makes the pancakes heavier. But whichever ones you choose, remember to serve them with lashings of syrup.

orange cornmeal hotcakes with orange flower syrup

⅔ cup/150 ml buttermilk

2 eggs, separated

3 tablespoons freshly squeezed orange juice

finely grated zest of ½ orange

½ cup/50 g cornmeal or polenta

½ cup/50 g all-purpose/plain flour

1 teaspoon baking powder

3 tablespoons soft brown sugar

a pinch of salt

melted butter, for greasing and to serve

orange flower syrup

½ cup/125 ml maple syrup

a drop of orange flower water

serves 4

Preheat the oven to low.

To make the orange flower syrup, stir the maple syrup and orange flower water together in a small bowl.

Put the buttermilk, egg yolks, and orange juice and zest in a mixing bowl and beat together. Add the cornmeal, flour, baking powder, sugar, and salt and fold in until just moistened. Do not overmix or you will toughen the texture.

Whisk the egg whites in a separate bowl with an electric handheld whisk until soft peaks form. Using a large metal spoon, fold the whites into the batter.

Wipe a skillet with a piece of kitchen paper dipped in melted butter. Heat up, then drop in 2–3 tablespoons of the batter. Cook for 2 minutes, until bubbles appear on the top and the edges are dry. Cook in batches of 3 or whatever fits comfortably in your skillet. Flip the hotcakes over and cook for 2 minutes on the other side. Keep warm in the oven while you make the rest. Serve about 3 hotcakes per person. Put some melted butter on each hotcake and serve with the orange flower syrup.

blueberry pancakes

1 cup/125 g self-rising flour

1 teaspoon baking powder

2 tablespoons sugar

¼ teaspoon salt

1 egg

⅓ cup/100 ml whole milk

3 tablespoons butter, melted

1 cup/150 g blueberries, plus extra to serve

maple syrup, to serve

serves 4

Preheat the oven to low.

Sift the flour and baking powder into a mixing bowl and stir in the sugar and salt. Put the egg, milk, and ⅓ cup/75 ml water in a pitcher/jug and beat to combine.

Stir half the butter into the wet ingredients in the pitcher/jug. Mix the wet ingredients with the dry ingredients until no lumps of flour remain.

Wipe a heavy-based skillet with a scrunched-up piece of kitchen paper dipped in the remaining melted butter. Heat up, then drop in 4 tablespoons of the batter. Cook for 1–2 minutes on the first side, then scatter over a few of the blueberries and flip the pancake over. Cook for 2 minutes, until golden and cooked through. Keep warm in the oven while you make the rest. Serve with more blueberries and lashings of maple syrup.

As dairy-free pancakes can't contain egg, they are a bit more dense. However, as they are drenched in a runny lime and honey syrup, this is soon taken care of. Try to find the ripest, most perfumed mango to make this dish exquisite. Or, if banana is your preferred fruit, try the buckwheat pancakes. The bananas caramelize in the hot pan, and when you drizzle over some honey before serving, everything becomes even sweeter.

dairy-free coconut pancakes with lime syrup & mango

1¼ cups/150 g all-purpose/plain flour

3 teaspoons baking powder

¼ teaspoon salt

2 tablespoons brown sugar

3 tablespoons dried shredded/desiccated coconut

¾ cup/200 ml coconut milk

2 tablespoons safflower/sunflower oil, plus extra for frying

1 mango, peeled, pitted and sliced

lime syrup

freshly squeezed juice of 3 limes

grated zest of 1 lime

½ cup/100 g clear honey

6 cardamom pods, crushed

serves 4

Preheat the oven to low.

To make the lime syrup, put the lime juice and zest, honey, and cardamom pods in a small saucepan and bring to the boil. Boil for 5 minutes, then remove from the heat and set aside.

Meanwhile, sift the flour, baking powder, and salt into a large mixing bowl and stir in the sugar and coconut. Put the coconut milk, ¼ cup/75 ml water and the oil in a pitcher/jug and beat to combine. Mix the wet ingredients with the dry ingredients until no lumps of flour remain.

Heat a heavy-based skillet over medium heat. Grease the pan with a piece of kitchen paper dipped in oil. Drop 2–3 tablespoons of batter into the pan. Cook for 1–2 minutes on each side until golden and cooked through. Keep warm in the oven while you make the rest. Serve with mango and lime syrup.

buckwheat & banana pancakes

½ cup/75 g buckwheat flour

⅓ cup/40 g all-purpose/plain flour

1 teaspoon baking soda/bicarbonate of soda

¼ teaspoon salt

2 tablespoons clear honey, plus extra to serve

2 eggs, separated

1 cup/250 ml sour cream

safflower/sunflower oil, for frying

2 bananas, sliced

serves 4

Preheat the oven to low.

Sift the flours, baking soda and salt into a large mixing bowl. Put the honey, egg yolks, and sour cream in a picher/jug and beat to combine. Mix the wet ingredients with the dry ingredients until no lumps of flour remain.

Whisk the egg whites in a separate bowl with an electric handheld whisk until soft peaks form. Using a large metal spoon, fold the whites into the batter.

Heat a heavy-based skillet over medium heat. Grease the skillet with a piece of kitchen paper dipped in oil. Drop 2–3 tablespoons of batter into the skillet. Cook for 1–2 minutes on the first side, until the edges look dry, then scatter over 3–4 slices of banana and flip the pancake over. Cook for 2 minutes, until golden and cooked through. Keep warm in the oven while you make the rest. Serve with honey, for drizzling.

Two fruity, healthy breakfasts to start the day: a quick and easy way to serve zingy grapefruit. If you don't have a grapefruit knife, a small paring knife does a good job too. And a delicious fruit compote served with seeds and plain yogurt. Both taste far more indulgent than they really are!

pink grapefruit with vanilla sugar

2 pink grapefruits

1 vanilla bean/pod, split lengthwise

2 tablespoons sugar

plain yogurt, to serve (optional)

serves 2

Halve the grapefruits and slice a little off each top and bottom so they sit securely on a flat surface. Loosen the flesh from the shell with a curved grapefruit knife or small paring knife. (It is important to do this at this stage as trying to do this when the grapefruit is hot can be quite dangerous.)

Scrape the seeds out of the vanilla bean/pod and add to the sugar. Mix thoroughly with the back of a spoon to spread out the seeds.

Preheat the broiler/grill.

Place the grapefruit halves on a baking sheet, flesh side up, and sprinkle the sugar over them. Slide under the broiler/grill and let the sugar melt and caramelize. It should only take 2–3 minutes. Remove from under the broiler and leave to cool for 2 minutes. Serve with plain yogurt on the side or by itself, if preferred.

spiced pear, apricot, & fig compote

⅔ cup/150 ml unsweetened apple juice

1 cup/100 g ready-to-eat dried apricots, halved

½ cup/50 g ready-to-eat dried figs, halved

8 cardamom pods, lightly crushed

2 pears, cored and sliced into wedges

3½ oz./100 g low-fat Greek yogurt, to serve

2 teaspoons pumpkin seeds, to serve

serves 2

Put all the ingredients in a saucepan, bring to a simmer and cook, covered, for 2–4 minutes, depending on the ripeness of the pears. Transfer to a bowl and let cool. Cover and chill overnight in the refrigerator.

To serve, discard the cardamom pods and divide the compote between two serving bowls. Top each bowlful with half of the Greek yogurt and 1 teaspoon of pumpkin seeds.

If when it comes to choosing between eating breakfast or an extra five minutes in bed, you choose the extra five minutes, Morning Muffins are the breakfast for you! Simply grab one from an airtight container as you head out of the door and you have a healthy, filling breakfast that can be eaten on the move. On the occasions you have some time to spare, try this quick and tasty porridge, which is uplifted by fresh raspberries.

morning muffins

6 oz./170 g ready-to-eat dried apricots, coarsely chopped

1 cup/170 g unsweetened muesli

2 cups/250 g self-rising flour

1 teaspoon baking powder

1 cup/250 ml unsweetened apple juice

3 tablespoons vegetable oil

1/3 cup/100 ml clear honey

1 large egg

a 12-hole muffin pan, lined with 12 paper muffin cases

makes 12

Put the apricots, muesli, flour, and baking powder in a large mixing bowl and stir. In a separate bowl, mix the apple juice, oil, honey, and egg. Fold into the dry ingredients, but do not overmix.

Spoon the mixture into the paper muffin cases. Bake in a preheated oven at 375°F (190°C) Gas 5 for 20 minutes, until golden and risen. Remove from the oven and serve immediately, or transfer to a wire rack to cool. Store in an airtight container for up to 3 days.

Variation: Add the finely grated zest of 1 unwaxed orange and replace the apple juice with freshly squeezed orange juice. Include the little shreds of orange flesh obtained from squeezing the fruit.

cinnamon porridge

2/3 cup/80 g whole rolled oats

2 tablespoons wheatgerm

1 teaspoon ground cinnamon

1¼ cup/300 ml skimmed milk

a pinch of salt

4 tablespoons whole almonds, chopped

1 cup/100 g fresh raspberries

1 medium banana, sliced

4 teaspoons maple syrup or clear honey, to serve

serves 2

Put the oats, wheatgerm, and cinnamon in a saucepan, then add the milk, salt, and a scant ½ cup/100 ml of water. Cook over medium heat for about 5 minutes or until the oats are tender and the porridge has thickened.

Pour the porridge into a bowl and top with the almonds, raspberries, and banana, then drizzle the maple syrup or honey over the top to serve.

Eggs are a great start to the day, but if you fancy something different from usual scrambled, fried, or boiled, try one of these variations. Softly poached eggs with spicy tomato sauce or baked eggs with fresh spinach make these great brunch options.

huevos rancheros

1 tablespoon soy sauce

1 onion, chopped

1 green bell pepper, seeded and chopped

1 red chile, seeded and finely chopped

1 garlic clove, crushed

1 teaspoon ground cumin

14-oz./400-g can chopped tomatoes

2 very fresh eggs

sea salt and freshly ground black pepper

2 tablespoons chopped fresh cilantro/coriander, to serve

4 slices of whole-grain toast, to serve

serves 2

Heat the soy sauce and 2 tablespoons of water in a non-stick skillet. Add the onion and cook for 5 minutes until the liquid has evaporated and the onion has softened. Stir in the pepper, chile, garlic, and ground cumin and cook for 1 minute.

Tip in the tomatoes, season, and simmer, uncovered, for 5 minutes until the sauce has thickened. Make 2 hollows in the sauce and break an egg into each one. Reduce the heat, cover the skillet, and cook for 5 minutes until the eggs are soft set. Scatter with cilantro/coriander and serve with 2 slices of whole-grain toast per serving.

Florentine baked eggs

8 oz./225 g young leaf spinach, rinsed

freshly grated nutmeg

4 very fresh eggs

4 dessertspoons virtually fat-free sour cream or fromage frais

2 tablespoons freshly grated Parmesan cheese

sea salt and freshly ground black pepper

8 slices of whole-grain toast, to serve

4 ramekins, lightly greased

a small roasting pan

serves 4

Put the kettle on to boil. Cook the spinach in a covered saucepan until wilted, stirring once or twice. Drain off any excess liquid and season with nutmeg, salt and pepper to taste.

Divide the spinach between the prepared ramekins. Make a hollow in the spinach and break an egg into each one. Season lightly, then top each egg with a spoonful of sour cream/fromage frais and a sprinkling of Parmesan cheese.

Put the ramekins in the roasting pan and pour boiling water around them to come halfway up the sides. Bake in a preheated oven at 350°F (180°C) Gas 4 for 14–16 minutes, depending on how soft you like the yolks. Bear in mind that the eggs will carry on cooking after they have come out of the oven. Serve immediately with 2 slices of whole-grain toast per serving.

These two egg dishes are packed with so much flavor, they make great brunch dishes that will really wake you up. The delicious, golden tortilla is given a kick with a little chile, while the fritters are made from handfuls of fragrant fresh herbs. Sumac, is a wild berry which, when dried and ground, adds a sour tang to food, a little like lemon juice.

tortilla with potatoes, chiles, & piquillo peppers

6 tablespoons olive oil

1¼ lb./600 g (about 4) potatoes, peeled and thinly sliced

2 red chiles, thinly sliced

1 onion, thinly sliced

½ teaspoon sea salt

8 eggs

4½ oz./125 g marinated (jarred) roasted piquillo peppers/pimentos, drained and sliced

a 8-inch/20-cm non-stick frying pan, at least 3 inch/ 7 cm deep

serves 6

Heat 4 tablespoons of the oil in the skillet, then add the potatoes, chiles, onion, and salt. Reduce the heat to low and cover with a lid. Cook for 15 minutes, stirring occasionally so the onions don't catch on the skillet base.

Preheat the broiler/grill to medium heat.

Beat the eggs in a large mixing bowl. Transfer the cooked ingredients from the skillet to the beaten eggs and stir. Add the roasted piquillo peppers/pimentos.

Turn the heat up to medium under the skillet and add the remaining oil. Pour the egg mixture into the skillet. Cook for 4–5 minutes until the base is golden—loosen the sides and lift up to check.

Broil/grill for 3–4 minutes, until it is cooked all the way through. Cut into wedges to serve.

herb fritters with fried eggs & sumac tomatoes

4 or 5 plum tomatoes, roughly chopped

2 teaspoons ground sumac

3 tablespoons extra virgin olive oil

5 extra-large eggs

1 teaspoon ground cumin

2 big handfuls of fresh flat-leaf parsley, leaves

roughly chopped and stalks discarded

1 small handful fresh cilantro/coriander, leaves roughly chopped and stalks discarded

sea salt and freshly ground black pepper

serves 4

Preheat the oven to low.

Put the tomatoes and sumac in a bowl with 1 tablespoon of the oil. Season and toss until coated, then set aside.

Crack one egg into a mixing bowl, season, add the cumin, and beat to mix. Stir in the herbs. It will look like there is not enough egg, but you only need enough to bind it.

Heat a skillet over high heat and add 1 tablespoon of the oil. Drop 2 tablespoons of the herb mixture in the skillet to make your first fritter and continue until you run out of space in the skillet. Cook over high heat for 2 minutes on each side, until lightly golden. Keep warm in the oven while you fry the rest.

Once all the fritters are done, add the remaining oil to the same skillet and wait for it to heat up. Crack the remaining 4 eggs into the skillet, being careful to keep the yolks intact, and fry for 2 minutes. Cover with a lid and cook for a further 30–40 seconds just to cook the top of the whites; you want the egg yolk to remain runny.

Divide the fritters between 4 plates, top with a fried egg and scatter the sumac tomatoes over the top.

Poached eggs served with spinach and spiced butter is a dish that has it's origins in Turkish cuisine. It is a meal packed with so much flavor that you will be hooked from the first taste. If you can't get hold of Turkish bread then pita or soughdough work well too.

hash browns

2 tablespoons butter

1 onion, chopped

1¼ lb./600 g large potatoes, peeled and grated

1 egg white, beaten

vegetable oil, for deep-frying

sea salt and freshly ground black pepper

makes 16

Heat the butter in a frying pan, then add the onion, cover with a lid and cook over low heat until soft.

Put the potatoes into a large mixing bowl and stir in the softened onions. Stir in the egg white and season generously with salt and pepper.

Fill a large saucepan one-third full with vegetable oil. Heat to 190°C (or until a blob of the potato mixture browns within a few seconds).

Roll the potato mixture into walnut-sized balls, then flatten slightly before adding to the hot oil. Fry in batches of 4–5 for 2–3 minutes, until golden brown. Drain on paper towels and serve with extra salt, for sprinkling.

poached eggs on spinach with yogurt & spiced butter

1 small garlic clove, crushed

7 oz./200 g Greek yogurt

1 loaf of Turkish flat bread, cut into 4 squares and halved horizontally

3 tablespoons butter

½ teaspoon cumin seeds

½ teaspoon dried hot pepper/chilli flakes

½ teaspoon sea salt flakes

1 tablespoon olive oil

14 oz./400 g spinach

8 extra-large eggs

sea salt and freshly ground black pepper

serves 4

Preheat the broiler/grill to high.

Get everything ready before you start cooking: mix the garlic and yogurt. Put the flat bread on a baking sheet. Put the butter, cumin, hot pepper/chilli flakes, and salt flakes in a small saucepan. Fill 2 deep skillets with water and bring to a boil over high heat.

Heat a wok, then add the olive oil and when hot, add the spinach in batches. Toss around the wok so it cooks evenly and when it is just wilted, take it off the heat, season to taste, and cover.

Reduce the heat under the 2 skillets to low so the water is barely simmering and break 4 eggs, far apart, into each pan. Leave for 3 minutes. Broil/grill the bread, cut side up, until lightly toasted, then transfer to 4 plates. Spread some garlic yogurt over the bread and heap a mound of spinach on top. Using a slotted spoon, sit a poached egg on top of each square of yogurty bread. Quickly heat the butter and spices over high heat until bubbling, pour over the eggs and serve immediately.

Toast can be served with an endless variety of toppings. Garlicky mushrooms are great for breakfast, but try them on a layer of soft, creamy goat cheese and you will be in utter heaven. Sweet, melting, roasted squash and tangy blue cheese are a sublime combination, too. For both dishes, seek out a good, sturdy rustic bread such as sourdough to prevent the underneath going soggy.

garlic mushrooms & goat cheese on sourdough toast

8 portobello mushrooms

3 garlic cloves, crushed

3 tablespoons olive oil

3 tablespoons pine nuts

2 tablespoons balsamic vinegar

4 slices of sourdough bread

5½ oz./150 g fresh goat cheese

sea salt and freshly ground black pepper

fresh tarragon, to serve

serves 4

Preheat the oven to 400°F (200°C) Gas 6.

Put the mushrooms, garlic, and oil in a roasting pan. Toss well and season. Roast in the preheated oven for 15 minutes, until tender. Stir in the pine nuts and balsamic vinegar halfway through roasting.

Just before the mushrooms are ready, toast the slices of sourdough bread and spread with the goat cheese. Place the mushrooms on top, stalk side up, scatter with the tarragon and serve immediately. Add more seasoning, if necessary.

butternut squash & blue cheese giant toasts

½ small butternut squash, about 14 oz./400 g

olive oil, for brushing

2 large, thick slices of rustic sourdough bread, or 4 smaller slices

3 oz./80 g blue cheese, such as Gorgonzola or dolcelatte

a handful of baby spinach leaves

sea salt and freshly ground black pepper

dressing

½ tablespoon balsamic vinegar

1 tablespoon olive oil

serves 2

Preheat the oven to 400°F (200°C) Gas 6.

Scoop the seeds out of the squash and cut the flesh lengthways into 4 wedges. Put in a baking dish, brush with olive oil and sprinkle with salt and pepper. Roast in the preheated oven for 45 minutes until tender, then remove from the oven and let cool slightly. When the squash is cool enough to handle, cut away the skin and discard.

To make the dressing, whisk the vinegar and oil in a small bowl and set aside.

Toast the bread on one side under a preheated grill, then turn it over. Arrange the squash on the untoasted side, put slices of the cheese on top and grill until the cheese is bubbling and the bread golden. Top each one with a handful of spinach leaves, pour over a few spoonfuls of the dressing, and serve.

snacks, appetizers, & salads

In colder weather, soups make a perfect warming snack or appetizer. Here are two classic French recipes. The Pumpkin Soup has potatoes added, which thicken it and smooth the strong, very sweet taste of pumpkin. The nutmeg is also a vital addition to serve. For the French Onion Soup, you need to get the caramelization of the onions spot on—cook them slowly and then, once soft, turn up the heat and cook until a sticky golden brown.

pumpkin soup

2¼ lbs./1 kg pumpkin, preferably green or grey-skinned, peeled, deseeded and cut into large chunks

2 large potatoes, quartered

4 cups/1 litre boiling vegetable stock

4 tablespoons/50 g unsalted butter

2 tablespoons olive oil

2 large onions, finely sliced

1 cup/250 ml milk

sea salt

4 tablespoons sour cream, to serve

freshly grated nutmeg, to serve

serves 4

Put the pumpkin and potatoes in a large saucepan, add enough vegetable stock to cover, then simmer until tender. Drain, reserving the cooking liquid.

Heat the butter and oil in a skillet, add the onions, and fry until softened and lightly golden. Transfer to a blender or food processor, then add the pumpkin and potatoes, in batches if necessary. Blend, adding enough milk and cooking liquid to make a thick purée.

Transfer the purée to a clean saucepan and stir in enough stock to make a thick, creamy soup. Add salt to taste, reheat without boiling, then ladle into heated soup bowls. Top with sour cream and nutmeg to serve.

Variations

Roasted pumpkin soup

Roast the pumpkin instead of boiling it, to give the soup a smoky taste.

Pumpkin, ginger, and coconut soup

Substitute coconut milk for the fresh milk and include ¾ inch/2 cm fresh ginger, sliced, and 2 crushed garlic cloves with the vegetables before boiling. Omit the nutmeg and serve sprinkled with freshly chopped cilantro/coriander leaves.

French onion soup

4 tablespoons/50 g butter

2¼ lbs./1 kg onions, sliced

2 garlic cloves, crushed

1 tablespoon sugar

2 tablespoons Cognac or brandy

1¼ cups/300 ml hard/dry apple cider

5 cups/1.2 litres vegetable stock

1 bouquet garni (1 sprig each of parsley, thyme and bay)

sea salt and freshly ground black pepper

garlic toasts

4 tablespoons extra virgin olive oil

1 garlic clove, crushed

1 small baguette or ½ large baguette, sliced

7 oz./200 g Gruyère cheese, grated

serves 4

Preheat the oven to 350°F (180°C) Gas 4.

To make the garlic toasts, mix the olive oil and garlic together and season well. Arrange the baguette slices on a baking sheet and brush with the garlic oil. Bake in the preheated oven for 20 minutes until crisp.

Melt the butter in a large saucepan or casserole dish over medium heat. Add the onions and garlic and stir until starting to soften. Turn the heat to low, cover and cook gently for 25–30 minutes until really softened. Take the lid off and add the sugar. Cook for a further 20 minutes, stirring until golden brown and extremely floppy-looking. This is the secret to a successful onion soup. Pour in the Cognac and cider and leave to bubble up for 1 minute. Add the stock and bouquet garni and stir to blend. Simmer for 45 minutes, then season. Remove the bouquet garni.

Preheat the broiler/grill. Divide the soup between 4 ovenproof bowls and place them on a baking sheet. Float 2–3 garlic toasts on top of each bowl and scatter the Gruyère over the toasts. Broil/grill until the Gruyère is bubbling and golden. Serve immediately using oven gloves.

Here are two variations on the classic crumbly puff pastry biscuit—both are delicious served with drinks. The extreme savoriness of both miso and Parmesan makes them a good flavor match. The caramelized onion option is more classic—and the onion mixture also sits nicely on an antipasti plate, or try it with mature Cheddar and crackers.

miso & Parmesan palmiers

13-oz./375-g sheet
ready-rolled puff pastry,
defrosted if frozen

2 tablespoons white
miso paste

4 tablespoons/50 g
unsalted butter, softened

1 oz./30 g Parmesan
cheese, finely grated

1 tablespoon toasted
sesame seeds

*a baking sheet lined with
baking parchment*

makes about 24

Lay the pastry on a clean work surface and allow it to defrost just enough so that it can be unrolled without cracking.

Combine the miso and butter in a small bowl and spread about two-thirds of this mixture evenly over the pastry. Sprinkle two-thirds of the Parmesan over the top. Fold the pastry in half lengthwise. Spread the remaining butter mixture on the pastry and sprinkle over the remaining cheese. Fold the pastry over again lengthwise to make a long rectangle shape and gently press down on the pastry. Put the pastry on the prepared baking sheet and then into the freezer for 30 minutes so that it can be cut easily.

When you are ready to cook the palmiers, preheat the oven to 400°F (200°C) Gas 6.

Using a sharp knife, cut the pastry into ½-inch/1-cm wide slices. Put the slices, cut-side up, on the baking sheet, sprinkle over the sesame seeds, and bake in the preheated oven for about 15 minutes, until puffed and golden. Serve while still warm.

caramelized onion palmiers

3 tablespoons olive oil

2 large white onions, very
thinly sliced

3 sprigs of fresh thyme

3 tablespoons soft brown
sugar

¼ cup/65 ml red wine

13-oz./375-g sheet
ready-rolled puff pastry,
defrosted if frozen

*a baking sheet lined with
baking parchment*

makes about 24

Put the oil in a heavy-based saucepan set over high heat. Add the onions and thyme. When the onions start to sizzle, reduce the heat to low, cover, and cook for 15 minutes, stirring often, until the onions start to caramelize and turn a golden color. Stir in the sugar and red wine and cook over medium heat until the liquid has been absorbed and the onions are thick and a deep plum color. Let cool.

Lay the pastry on a clean work surface and allow it to defrost just enough so that it can be unrolled without cracking.

Spread the onion mixture evenly over the pastry and loosely roll it up like a Swiss roll but do not roll it too tightly. Put it on the prepared baking sheet and then into the freezer for 30 minutes so that it can be cut easily.

When you are ready to cook the palmiers, preheat the oven to 400°F (200°C) Gas 6.

Using a sharp knife, cut the pastry into ½-inch/1-cm wide slices. Put the slices, cut-side up, on the baking sheet and bake in the preheated oven for about 15 minutes, until puffed and golden. Serve while still warm.

These topped breads are a wonderful mix of fresh spring flavors and colors and make a great start to a rustic summer meal. Puréeing the peas for the crostini gives a sweet, earthy base on which to sprinkle the combination of salty, nutty pecorino and fruity pears tossed in a few drops of balsamic vinegar for sharpness. Bocconcini (meaning "little bites") are tiny balls of mozzarella, but if you can't find them, dice regular mozzarella instead.

pear, pecorino, & pea crostini

1 thin French baguette, sliced into thin rounds

extra virgin olive oil, for brushing and moistening

9 oz./250 g shelled fresh or frozen peas

freshly grated nutmeg

1 small ripe pear

a drop balsamic or sherry vinegar

4½ oz./125 g fresh young pecorino or Parmesan cheese, diced

sea salt and freshly ground black pepper

serves 6

Preheat the oven to 375°F (190°C) Gas 5.

To make the crostini, brush both sides of each slice of bread with olive oil and spread out on a baking sheet. Bake for about 10 minutes until crisp and golden.

Meanwhile, blanch the peas in boiling water for 3 minutes if they are fresh or 2 minutes if they are frozen. Drain them, refresh in cold water and drain again. Purée the peas in a food processor or blender, moistening with a little olive oil. Season with salt, pepper, and freshly grated nutmeg. Core and finely chop the pear. Mix with a drop of balsamic or sherry vinegar, then add the cheese and mix well. Spread the crostini with a mound of pea purée and top with a spoonful of the pear and cheese mixture. Serve immediately.

cherry tomato, bocconcini, & basil bruschetta

4 tablespoons extra virgin olive oil

1 teaspoon balsamic vinegar

12 bocconcini cheeses, halved, or 13 oz./375 g regular mozzarella cheese, cubed

20 ripe cherry tomatoes or pomodorini (baby plum tomatoes), halved

a handful of torn fresh basil leaves, plus extra to serve

4½ oz./125 g arugula/rocket leaves

sea salt and freshly ground black pepper

bruschetta

4 thick slices country bread, preferably sourdough

2 garlic cloves, halved

extra virgin olive oil, for sprinkling

serves 4

Whisk 3 tablespoons of the olive oil with the balsamic vinegar. Season to taste with salt and pepper. Stir in the halved bocconcini or mozzarella cubes, tomatoes and torn basil leaves.

To make the bruschetta, broil/grill, toast, or pan-grill the bread on both sides until lightly charred or toasted. Rub the top side of each slice with the cut garlic, then drizzle with olive oil.

Cover each slice of bruschetta with arugula/rocket and spoon over the tomatoes and mozzarella. Sprinkle with the remaining olive oil and top with fresh basil leaves.

Here are two deliciously simple recipes, both ideal for the warmer months. Using ready-made puff pastry dough is quick and easy but topped with fresh asparagus and creamy goat cheese it makes an elegant and impressive tart. Just as easy to make is baked ricotta, and as it can be eaten warm or cold, you can serve it freshly made as an appetizer and then enjoy any leftovers the following day as a light lunch.

asparagus & goat cheese tart

2 x 13-oz./375-g sheets ready-rolled puff pastry, defrosted if frozen

1 egg, lightly beaten and mixed with 2 teaspoons water

2 tablespoons butter

2 tablespoons light olive oil

2 bunches thin asparagus, woody ends trimmed

5½ oz./150 g soft goat cheese

sea salt and freshly ground black pepper

lightly dressed salad leaves, to serve (optional)

2 baking sheets, lined with baking parchment

serves 4–6

Preheat the oven to 425°F (220°C) Gas 7. Cut the sheets of pastry to make two rectangles 10 x 5 inch/24 x 12 cm and place each one on a prepared baking sheet. Cut ½-inch/1-cm wide strips from the remaining pastry. Brush around the edges of the pastry rectangles and place the strips on the edges to form a border. Prick each pastry sheet all over with a fork and brush the beaten egg over it. Cook in the preheated oven for 15 minutes, until pale golden and puffed.

Put the butter and olive oil in a skillet set over high heat and cook the asparagus for 2–3 minutes, turning often, until just beginning to soften. Season well with salt and pepper and set aside. Crumble the goat cheese over the pastry, being careful to stay within the borders. Top with the asparagus and cook in the preheated oven for a further 10 minutes, until the pastry is golden. Serve warm with lightly dressed salad greens, if liked.

baked ricotta with roasted cherry tomato salsa

1 lb./450 g ricotta cheese

½ teaspoon sea salt

1 egg, lightly beaten

1 oz./30 g Parmesan cheese, finely grated

¼ cup/60 ml olive oil

2 garlic cloves, sliced

12 cherry tomatoes, halved

1 tablespoon sherry vinegar

½ teaspoon sugar

10–12 fresh basil leaves, finely sliced

½ red onion, finely diced

sea salt and freshly ground black pepper

toasted sourdough bread, to serve (optional)

a 5-inch/12-cm square cake pan, lined with baking parchment

serves 4

Preheat the oven to 350°F (180°C) Gas 4.

Put the ricotta in a bowl with the salt, egg, and Parmesan and stir well. Spoon into the lined cake pan and bake in the preheated oven for 50 minutes. Remove from the oven and let cool before inverting onto a chopping board.

Put the olive oil in a skillet set over high heat and cook the garlic and tomatoes for 2 minutes, shaking the skillet, so that the tomatoes cook evenly and start to split and soften.

Remove from the heat, stir in the vinegar, sugar, basil, and onion and season to taste with salt and pepper.

Cut the baked ricotta into 4 thick slices and serve with the tomato salsa spooned over the top and the toasted sourdough on the side, if using.

Here is a delicious trio of creamy vegetable dips, which are great served with spelt toasts, or other artisanal breads. They are all made with root vegetables and are vibrantly colored, so make an attractive starter at a dinner party as well as a great, wholesome snack.

roasted parsnip & garlic dip

2 tablespoons chilled butter, cubed, plus extra for greasing
⅓ cup/90 ml heavy/double cream
½ teaspoon sea salt
¼ teaspoon white pepper
1 lb./500 g parsnips, peeled and sliced
1 garlic bulb, halved

serves 6–8

Preheat the oven to 350°F (180°C) Gas 4.

Lightly butter a small baking dish. Put the cream in a small bowl and stir in the salt and pepper.

Put the parsnips in the baking dish with the garlic. Pour the cream over the top, cover with foil, and cook in the preheated oven for 45 minutes. Remove the garlic from the dish and let cool. When cool enough to handle, squeeze the soft, baked garlic directly into the bowl of a food processor or blender and discard the skin. Add the remaining ingredients and process until smooth. Transfer to a serving dish and cover until ready to serve.

beet & caraway dip

3 medium beets/beetroot, uncooked
1 tablespoon horseradish sauce
⅓ cup/90 g sour cream
1 teaspoon caraway seeds
sea salt and white pepper

serves 6–8

Put the beets/beetroot in a large saucepan and cover with cold water. Bring to a boil and let boil for about 45–50 minutes, topping up the water from time to time, as necessary. They are ready when a skewer goes through them with little resistance. Drain and let cool. When cool enough to handle, peel the beets/beetroot and discard the skins. Roughly chop and put in a food processor or blender with the other ingredients and process until smooth. Season to taste, transfer to a serving dish, and cover until ready to serve.

spiced carrot dip

1 cup/250 ml vegetable stock
4 medium carrots, chopped
2 tablespoons light olive oil
1 small red onion, chopped
2 garlic cloves, chopped
1 large red chile, chopped
1 teaspoon fenugreek seeds
1 teaspoon ground cumin
sea salt and white pepper

serves 6–8

Put the stock in a saucepan and add the carrots, oil, onion, and garlic. Bring to a boil, then reduce the heat to low and simmer for 15–20 minutes, until almost all the liquid has evaporated and the carrots are soft. Add the chile, fenugreek, and cumin and stir-fry for 2–3 minutes.

Transfer the mixture to a food processor or blender and whizz until blended but still with a rough texture. Season to taste, transfer to a serving dish, and cover until ready to serve.

This summer grazing platter offers the best of the season's bounty—tasty little plates to nibble on during a summer's afternoon. The corn relish and pickled eggplant can be made a day in advance so the flavors have a chance to infuse, but the slow-roasted tomatoes are best served warm. Serve with fresh crusty bread and a generous slice of mature Cheddar.

corn relish

1 tablespoon olive oil
2 fresh ears of corn/corn-on-the-cobs, shucked
1 small red bell pepper, thinly sliced
1 small red onion, thinly sliced
1 garlic clove, finely chopped
1 tablespoon brown sugar
½ cup/125 ml vegetable stock
1 teaspoon cornstarch/cornflour
2 teaspoons hot English mustard
½ cup/125 ml cider vinegar

serves 4–6

Heat the oil in a skillet set over high heat and add the corn kernels, red bell pepper, and onion. Cook for 5 minutes, stirring constantly. Add the garlic and cook, stirring, for 1 minute. Stir in the sugar, add the stock, and bring to a boil. Reduce the heat and let simmer for about 10 minutes, until almost all the liquid has evaporated.

Put the cornstarch/cornflour, mustard, and vinegar in a small bowl and mix well. Add this mixture to the corn and cook over high heat for 1 minute, until the liquid thickens and coats the corn. Remove from the heat and let cool before serving.

pickled eggplant

1 cup/250 ml white wine vinegar
1 eggplant/aubergine, chopped
3 tablespoons olive oil
1 large red chile, sliced
½ teaspoon caraway seeds
1 garlic clove, sliced

serves 4–6

Put the vinegar in a small saucepan with 2 cups/500 ml water and bring to a boil. Add the eggplant/aubergine, cover with a lid, and turn off the heat. Let the eggplant/aubergine sit in the liquid for about 20 minutes. Drain well and let the eggplant/aubergine cool completely then put in a bowl with the oil, chile, caraway seeds, and garlic. Cover and refrigerate for 1 day before eating.

slow-roasted tomatoes

8 ripe Italian tomatoes, such as Roma, halved
1 tablespoon olive oil
½ teaspoon sea salt
½ teaspoon sugar
1 teaspoon ground cumin

serves 4–6

Preheat the oven to 350°F (180°C) Gas 4.

Put the tomatoes in a bowl with the other ingredients and toss to coat in the oil. Put the tomatoes, cut-side up, on a baking sheet and roast in the preheated oven for 1 hour, until they have shrivelled and are starting to char around the edges. Serve warm.

Salads should make the most of what is in season. Tomatoes and avocados are much better in the summertime and are ideally dressed very simply so their flavor shines through. This deliciously fresh spring salad includes a classic pairing of flavors—feta cheese and mint—and is perfect served with a cold glass of white wine on a warm day.

tomato, avocado, & lime salad with crisp tortillas

freshly squeezed juice of 1 lime, plus 1 lime

4 ripe, firm avocados

leaves from a large bunch of cilantro/coriander

6 tablespoons olive or avocado oil

24 small tomatoes, halved

2 garlic cloves, crushed

2 flour tortillas

sea salt and freshly ground black pepper

serves 6

Put the lime juice in a bowl. Cut the avocados in half, remove the stones, and peel. Cut each half into 4 wedges and toss with the lime juice.

Using a small paring knife, cut the top and bottom off of the lime. Cut away the skin and pith. Carefully slice between each segment and remove the flesh. Combine the lime flesh with the avocados, cilantro/coriander, 4 tablespoons of the oil, and tomatoes. Season to taste with salt and pepper and set aside.

Preheat the broiler/grill to hot.

In a small bowl, combine the garlic and remaining 2 tablespoons of oil. Brush the oil and garlic mixture over the tortillas and toast under the preheated broiler/grill for about 1 minute until brown.

Break the toasted tortillas into pieces and scatter over the salad just before serving.

feta, cucumber, & mint spring salad

2 mini cucumbers

6 breakfast radishes

2 good handfuls of arugula/rocket

a small handful of fresh mint leaves

5½ oz./150 g feta cheese, broken into small pieces

10–15 small black olives

ciabatta or other crusty bread, to serve

dressing

3 tablespoons extra virgin olive oil

1 tablespoon red wine vinegar

a good squeeze of lemon juice

sea salt and freshly ground black pepper

serves 2

To make the dressing, whisk or shake the ingredients together in a lidded jar.

Cut the cucumbers in half lengthwise and scoop out the seeds with the tip of a teaspoon. Slice lengthwise using a mandoline or vegetable peeler to make wafer-thin slices. Trim the radishes and thinly slice on the diagonal.

Put the arugula/rocket, mint, cucumber, and radishes in a bowl and toss together with the dressing. Add the crumbled feta and toss lightly again, then scatter over the olives. Divide the ingredients equally between 2 plates, piling them up in a mound. Serve with ciabatta or other crusty bread.

Panzanella is a classic Tuscan salad but can be given a decidedly Spanish edge with a few Iberian specialities thrown in, such as the Manchego cheese and the smoky paprika known as "pimentón de la Vera". For the salad, use soft white balls of mozzarella made from cow's or buffalo's milk (different from the firmer yellow variety used on pizza) and fragrant, fuzzy peaches.

Spanish-style panzanella

1 yellow bell pepper
6 ripe tomatoes, chopped
1 Spanish onion, thinly sliced into rings
1 large handful of flat leaf parsley leaves, roughly chopped
4 slices of sourdough bread, crusts removed
¼ cup/65 ml extra virgin olive oil

2 tablespoons sherry vinegar
½ teaspoon Spanish paprika
1 garlic clove, crushed
3½ oz./100 g Manchego cheese, shaved, to serve (optional)

a ridged stove-top grill/griddle pan

serves 4

Preheat the grill/griddle pan over high heat. Cook the bell pepper in the pan until the skin is blackened and puffed all over. Place in a clean plastic bag. When cool enough to handle, peel the pepper, discard the seeds and membrane, and slice the flesh. Put in a bowl with the tomatoes, onion, and parsley.

Toast the bread until golden. Tear each slice into 4–5 pieces and add to the bowl with the other ingredients.

Mix the olive oil, vinegar, paprika, and garlic in a bowl and pour over the salad, tossing everything to combine. Leave for 10 minutes before gently tossing through the cheese shavings, if using, to serve.

mozzarella, peach, & frisée salad

3 fresh peaches, cut into thin wedges
4 handfuls of frisée leaves, trimmed
1 large ball of buffalo mozzarella, torn into thin shreds

3 tablespoons extra virgin olive oil
1 tablespoon white wine vinegar
freshly ground black pepper

serves 4

Put the peach wedges and frisée in a large bowl and gently toss to mix. Arrange on a serving plate. Scatter the mozzarella pieces over the salad.

Put the olive oil, vinegar and black pepper in a bowl, whisk with a fork, and then spoon over the salad.

Variation

Replace the mozzarella with 5½ oz./150 g crumbled firm blue cheese and the frisée with spinach leaves. Or, alternatively, keep the mozzarella and replace the other ingredients with fresh slices of tomato, basil leaves, and some fruity extra virgin olive oil for a traditional Italian Insalata Caprese.

Here are two great vegetarian snacks or sides to have in your reportoire. Ratatouille is simply the best all-purpose summer dish there is—serve as a vegetable option or with rice or couscous as an entrée in itself. Tempura is perceived to be far more tricky than it is. Just follow a few simple rules: don't overbeat the batter, use crisp vegetables without too high a water content, and use iced water, which ensures the batter is light and lacy.

ratatouille

3 tablespoons olive oil

1 onion, sliced

3 garlic cloves, crushed

a small bunch of flat leaf parsley, chopped

1 large eggplant/aubergine, chopped

2–3 red and/or yellow bell peppers, seeded and chopped

4 zucchini/courgettes, sliced

¼ teaspoon sea salt

4 large tomatoes, skinned and chopped, OR a 14-oz./400-g can peeled plum tomatoes

2 teaspoons red wine vinegar or balsamic vinegar (optional)

sea salt and freshly ground black pepper

serves 6

Heat the oil in a large, heavy-based saucepan set over medium heat. Add the onion, garlic, and parsley and sauté for 10 minutes, stirring regularly.

Add the eggplant/aubergine and cook for 5 minutes. Add the bell peppers and zucchini/courgettes and stir in the salt. Cook for a few minutes, then add the tomatoes.

Cover and cook for 5 minutes until the tomatoes start to break down, then uncover and cook for 10–15 minutes until the vegetables are tender, adding a little water if necessary. Season to taste with vinegar, if using, and salt and pepper. Serve warm.

tempura of mixed veggies with citrus dipping sauce

8 asparagus spears, ends trimmed

1 yellow bell pepper, cut into ¼-inch/½-cm strips

1 red bell pepper, cut into ¼-inch/½-cm strips

2 cups/500 ml vegetable oil

6 tablespoons/50 g cornstarch/cornflour

1 cup/125 g all-purpose/plain flour

¼ teaspoon baking powder

½ teaspoon salt

1⅓ cups/325 ml iced water

citrus dipping sauce

¼ cup/65 ml Japanese soy sauce

1 tablespoon freshly squeezed lemon juice

1 tablespoon freshly squeezed lime juice

1 tablespoon freshly squeezed orange juice

serves 4

To make the citrus dipping sauce, put all of the ingredients in a small bowl and whisk to combine. Set aside until ready to serve.

Put the prepared vegetables on a plate near to your stove top. Put the oil in a skillet and set over medium/high heat. Combine the cornstarch/cornflour, flour, baking powder, and salt in a bowl. Put the iced water in another chilled bowl. Working quickly, add the flour mixture to the cold water, stirring for just a few seconds with a chopstick or a knife, leaving the mixture lumpy-looking.

Cook the tempura in batches. Add a small handful of vegetables to the batter, letting any excess batter drip back into the bowl. Cook for 2–3 minutes in the oil, turning often with tongs so that the batter cooks evenly all over and is lightly golden and lacy looking. Put the tempura on some kitchen paper for a minute to absorb any excess oil. Reheat the oil and repeat with the remaining vegetables and batter. Serve warm with the citrus dipping sauce on the side.

A couple of potato dishes to try instead of the usual roasties. The harissa potatoes have the virtue of cooking on top of the stove—useful when you're making a roast and oven space is limited. The salt-baked spuds are so nice that you can make a meal of them, using them like bread alongside a bountiful cheese tray and a mixed green salad.

new potatoes baked with sea salt

coarse sea salt

a few sprigs of fresh thyme

2 lb./1 kg baby new potatoes, scrubbed but unpeeled

an ovenproof pan with a lid

serves 4

Preheat the oven to 425°F (220°C) Gas 7.

The amount of salt will depend on the size of your cooking vessel. Choose a shallow ovenproof pan with a tight-fitting lid. The salt should be spread in a layer about 1-inch/3 cm thick. Dot with the sprigs of thyme, then arrange the potatoes on top in a single layer. Don't bury them in the salt—they cook on top.

Cover with a lid and bake in the preheated oven at until the potatoes are tender when pierced with a knife, 35–45 minutes. Remove from the oven and set aside, covered, 5–10 minutes. To serve, remove the potatoes and brush off any salt. Serve hot.

harissa potatoes

3 tablespoons extra virgin olive oil

1 onion, sliced

1⅔ lb./750 g potatoes, thickly sliced

5 garlic cloves, sliced

1 heaped teaspoon harissa, or more to taste

1 teaspoon ground cumin

1 teaspoon coarse sea salt

1 tablespoon freshly squeezed lemon juice

a large handful of fresh cilantro/coriander, chopped

sea salt and freshly ground black pepper

serves 4

Heat the oil in a large sauté pan with a lid. Add the onion and cook for 1 minute, then add the potatoes and cook for 2–3 minutes more, stirring often. Add the garlic, harissa, cumin, and salt and mix well. Add enough water to cover by half, then cover with a lid and simmer gently for 20 minutes.

Uncover and continue simmering until the potatoes are cooked through and the liquid has been almost completely absorbed, 5–8 minutes more. Stir in the lemon juice and the cilantro/coriander, add salt and pepper to taste, and serve.

quick meals

Omelets, and their Italian cousins, frittatas are a great stand-by for a no-fuss, fast supper, or even a weekend brunch. The omelet has a distinctly Asian feel with creamy cubes of tofu replacing the more traditional cheese. Crunchy asparagus and corn work nicely in the frittata combined with farm-fresh eggs, creamy goat cheese, and fresh, tangy dill.

tenderstem broccoli, shiitake, & tofu omelet

1 tablespoon light olive oil

2 shallots, sliced

1 bunch of tenderstem broccoli, chopped into small pieces

7 oz./200 g shiitake mushrooms

1¾ oz./50 g baby spinach leaves

2 teaspoons light soy sauce

10½ oz./300 g firm tofu, cubed

8 eggs, lightly beaten

ground white pepper

oyster sauce, to serve (optional)

serves 4

Put the oil in a large, non-stick skillet and set over high heat. Add the shallots, broccoli, and mushrooms and stir-fry for 3–4 minutes, until the mushrooms are soft and the broccoli turns a bright, emerald green. Add the spinach and cook until just wilted. Add the soy sauce and stir. Arrange the cubes of tofu over the vegetables so that they are evenly spaced. Preheat the broiler/grill to high. Pour the beaten eggs into the skillet and cook over high heat until the edges have puffed up.

Keep the omelet in the skillet, place it under the preheated broiler/grill and cook until golden and firm on top. Remove and let cool a little before drizzling with the oyster sauce (if using), then sprinkle with white pepper to serve.

Variation

Replace the broccoli with young, tender peas and add a sprinkling of fresh cilantro/coriander.

asparagus, corn, & goat cheese frittata

2 bunches of thin asparagus spears

4 tablespoons/50 g butter

4 scallions/spring onions, finely chopped

2 fresh ears of corn/corn-on-the-cobs, shucked

1 handful of fresh dill, chopped

8 eggs, beaten

7 oz./200 g firm goat cheese, broken into pieces

sea salt and freshly ground black pepper

serves 4

Trim, or snap off, the woody ends from the asparagus and cut the spears into 1-inch/3-cm pieces.

Heat half of the butter in a large non-stick skillet set over medium heat. Add the asparagus, scallions/spring onions, and corn, and fry for 2–3 minutes, stirring often. Transfer the vegetables to a large bowl and add the dill, reserving a little to use as garnish. Wipe the pan clean. Add the beaten eggs to the vegetables, gently stirring to combine, and season well with salt and pepper.

Preheat the broiler/grill to high. Put the remaining butter in the skillet and set over high heat. Swirl the skillet around as the butter melts so that it coats the bottom and just starts to sizzle. Pour the frittata mixture into the skillet and reduce the heat to medium. Arrange the pieces of goat cheese over the top of the frittata and gently push them into the mixture. Cook for about 8 minutes, until the sides of the frittata start to puff up (reduce the heat if the bottom appears to be cooking too quickly).

Keep the fritatta in the skillet and place it under the preheated broiler/grill. Cook for 1 minute only just to set the top. Let cool a little in the skillet, sprinkle with the reserved dill, and serve immediately.

This is simple tapas-style food at its best. The tortilla may not look that substantial, but thanks to the creamy Taleggio cheese, it packs a super-rich taste punch and is more than enough for four to enjoy as a starter or snack. The red bell pepper tapenade is a very versatile recipe to have in your repertoire as it can also be tossed through cooked pasta or stirred into soup.

Taleggio & potato tortilla with red bell pepper tapenade

10–12 small, waxy new potatoes, thickly sliced

1 small red onion, roughly chopped

1 tablespoon olive oil

1 cup/250 ml vegetable stock

1 handful of fresh flat leaf parsley, chopped

3½ oz./100 g Taleggio cheese, chopped or torn into large chunks

2 eggs, lightly beaten

red pepper tapenade

1 large red bell pepper

1 garlic clove, chopped

⅓ cup/50 g pine nuts, lightly toasted

2 tablespoons olive oil

2 oz./50 g Parmesan cheese, finely grated

serves 4

To make the tapenade, preheat the oven to 425°F (220°C) Gas 7. Put a baking sheet in the oven for a few minutes to heat. Put the red bell pepper on the sheet and cook it in the preheated oven for about 15 minutes, turning often until the skin is starting to blacken and puff up. Transfer it to a clean plastic bag and let cool. When the bell pepper is cool enough to handle, peel off the skin, roughly tear or chop the flesh, and put it in a food processor. Add the garlic, pine nuts, and oil and process until smooth. Spoon into a bowl, add the Parmesan, and stir well to combine.

Put the potatoes, onion, and oil in a skillet and cook for 1 minute over high heat. Add the stock and cook for about 10 minutes, until the stock has evaporated and the vegetables start to sizzle in the skillet. Stir through the parsley and put the pieces of cheese among the potatoes. Pour the eggs into the skillet and cook for 2–3 minutes until they start to puff up around the edges. Give the skillet a couple of firm shakes—this will make it easier to get the cooked tortilla out.

Meanwhile, preheat the broiler/grill to high. Put the skillet under the hot broiler/grill and cook the tortilla for 1–2 minutes, until the top is golden but still wobbly in the centre. Use a spatula to smear some of the tapenade onto the base of a serving plate and carefully slide the tortilla onto the plate. Cut into 4 slices and eat direct from the plate with extra tapenade on the side.

Basil oil is particularly good sprinkled onto this simple pastry, but you can use ordinary olive oil. Preheating the baking sheet will make the base of the tart beautifully crisp.

simple tomato & olive tart with Parmesan

12 oz./350 g sheet ready-rolled puff pastry, defrosted if frozen

4½ oz./125 g red cherry tomatoes, halved

4½ oz./125 g yellow cherry tomatoes, halved

⅓ cup/50 g semi-dried or sun-dried tomatoes, halved

⅓ cup/50 g pitted black olives, halved

2 tablespoons basil oil (below)

1 oz./25 g Parmesan cheese, shaved

sea salt and freshly ground black pepper

a handful of arugula/rocket leaves, to serve

basil oil

1 oz./25 g fresh basil leaves

⅔ cup/150 ml extra virgin olive oil

a pinch of sea salt

2 baking sheets

serves 4

To make the basil oil, blanch the leaves very briefly in boiling water, drain, and dry thoroughly with kitchen paper. Put into a blender, add the oil and salt and blend until very smooth. Strain the oil through a fine strainer/sieve, or one lined with cheesecloth/muslin. Keep in the refrigerator but return to room temperature before use.

Preheat the oven to 425°F (220°C) Gas 7 and put a baking sheet on the middle shelf.

Roll out the dough on a lightly floured surface to form a rectangle, 10 x 12 inch/25 x 30 cm. Trim the edges and transfer the dough to a second baking sheet. Using the blade of a sharp knife, gently tap the edges several times (this will help the pastry rise and the edges separate) and prick all over with a fork.

Put the tomatoes, olives, a few tablespoons of the basil oil, salt, and pepper into a bowl and mix lightly. Spoon the mixture over the dough and carefully slide the tart directly onto the preheated baking sheet. Bake for 12–15 minutes until risen and golden.

Remove from the oven and sprinkle with the Parmesan. Cut into 4 and serve hot with the arugula/rocket leaves.

Crumbly goat cheese works surprisingly well in pesto, adding a slightly creamy edge to it. Roughly crumble it in so you get pockets of the molten cheese tucked in amongst the tangle of tagliatelle.

tagliatelle with peas & goat cheese pesto

9 oz./250 g fresh or frozen peas, defrosted
14 oz./400 g tagliatelle, fresh or dried
sea salt and freshly ground black pepper
freshly grated Parmesan cheese, to serve

goat cheese pesto
1 small garlic clove
2 large green chiles, seeded
2 handfuls fresh basil leaves,
plus extra to serve
3 tablespoons pine nuts
⅓ cup/100 ml extra virgin olive oil
3½ oz./100 g goat cheese

serves 4

To make the pesto, put the garlic, chiles, basil, and a large pinch of salt in a food processor and process until roughly chopped. Alternatively, crush everything with a pestle and mortar.

Put the pine nuts in a dry skillet and toast over low heat for a few minutes, shaking the pan, until they are golden all over. Add the pine nuts to the mixture in the food processor (or the mortar) and process again until coarsely chopped. Add half the olive oil and process again. Add the remaining oil, crumble in the goat cheese, and stir. Taste and season.

Bring a large saucepan of salted water and a small saucepan of unsalted water to a boil. Add the peas to the smaller pan and simmer for 4–5 minutes if fresh or 3 minutes if frozen. Once the water in the large pan comes to a rolling boil, add the tagliatelle and cook according to the manufacturer's instructions if dried, or for 2–3 minutes if fresh, until it is al dente. Drain and tip back into the pan.

Add 2–3 good dollops of pesto and the peas to the tagliatelle and toss through the hot strands, then add the remaining pesto making sure all the pasta is thoroughly coated. Transfer to bowls and sprinkle with basil and freshly grated Parmesan.

Here are two recipes for tasty, international dishes that can be on the table in less than 30 minutes. In this cheat's biryani the vegetables are stir-fried with a spicy curry paste and then the cooked rice is added. Roasting vegetables in the oven first makes easy work of a pasta sauce. The veggies soften and sweeten while they cook and there is no constant stirring involved as there is with stove-top cooking.

lime pickle & vegetable biryani

2 tablespoons lime pickle

1 onion, roughly chopped

2 garlic cloves

2 teaspoons grated fresh ginger

2 tablespoons olive oil

2 carrots, cut into thin batons

2 zucchini/courgettes, cut into thin batons

1¾ cups/370 g basmati rice

2 oz./50 g dried rice vermicelli, broken into shorter lengths (optional)

a large handful of fresh mint leaves, larger leaves roughly torn

⅓ cup/50 g toasted cashews, roughly chopped

serves 4

Put the pickle, onion, garlic, and ginger in a food processor and process to make a paste.

Heat the oil in a large, heavy-based saucepan set over medium heat. Add the paste and cook, stirring, for 2–3 minutes, until aromatic. Add the carrots and stir-fry for 2–3 minutes, until lightly golden. Add the zucchini/courgettes and stir-fry for 2 minutes, then turn off the heat.

Bring a large saucepan of water to a boil. Add the rice and cook for 8–10 minutes, until just tender. Add the rice vermicelli, if using, and cook for another 2–3 minutes, stirring well so that the vermicelli does not stick together and is soft and transparent. Drain well.

Set the saucepan with the vegetables over high heat. Add the rice mixture and stir well until it takes on the golden color of the curry paste. Stir in the mint and scatter with toasted cashews to serve.

pappardelle pasta with roast fennel, tomato, & olives

¼ cup/65 ml extra virgin olive oil

4 tomatoes, halved

2 red onions, cut into wedges

4 small zucchini/courgettes, thickly sliced

2 small fennel bulbs, thickly sliced

2 garlic cloves, thickly sliced

1 teaspoon smoked paprika (pimentón)

⅓ cup/50 g small black olives

14 oz./400 g fresh pappardelle pasta

2 tablespoons butter

salt and freshly ground black pepper

grated Manchego cheese, to serve

serves 4

Preheat the oven to 425°F (220°C) Gas 7.

Put the olive oil in a roasting pan and put it in the oven for 5 minutes to heat up.

Add all of the vegetables and the garlic to the roasting pan and sprinkle over the paprika. Season to taste with salt and pepper. Roast in the preheated oven for about 20 minutes, giving the pan a shake after 15 minutes. Remove from the oven and stir in the olives. Cover and let sit while you cook the pasta.

Bring a large saucepan of lightly salted water to a boil. Add the pasta and cook according to the package instructions, or just until the pasta rises to the top—it will cook much quicker than dried pasta. Drain well and return to the warm pan. Add the butter and toss well. Add the roasted vegetables and toss gently to combine. Sprinkle with grated Manchego to serve.

For delicious quick meals, take short cuts to make your life easier. This is a cheat's curry because it uses a ready-made curry paste. To lift your stir-fries out of the ordinary and into the sublime, you can be a bit crafty with ingredients. Both lemongrass and kaffir lime leaves can be tricky to find, but they freeze well so keep a few stored in the freezer for meals such as this.

quick vegetable curry

3 tablespoons peanut/groundnut oil or safflower/sunflower oil

1 onion, sliced

2 garlic cloves, chopped

1 inch/2.5 cm piece fresh ginger, peeled and grated

1 tablespoon hot curry paste

1 teaspoon ground cinnamon

1 lb./500 g baking potatoes, cut into cubes

14-oz./400-g can chopped tomatoes

1¼ cups/300 ml vegetable stock (page 162)

1 tablespoon tomato paste/purée

7 oz./200 g button mushrooms, halved

7 oz./200 g frozen peas

⅓ cup/25 g ground almonds

2 tablespoons chopped fresh cilantro/coriander

sea salt and freshly ground black pepper

basmati rice, to serve

serves 4

Heat the oil in a saucepan and fry the onion, garlic, ginger, curry paste, and cinnamon for 5 minutes. Add the potatoes, tomatoes, stock, tomato paste/purée, salt, and pepper. Bring to a boil, cover, and simmer gently for 20 minutes.

Add the mushrooms, peas, ground almonds, and cilantro/coriander to the pan and cook for a further 10 minutes. Taste and adjust the seasoning with salt and pepper, then serve with basmati rice.

stir-fried vegetables & tofu with lime leaves & honey

1 tablespoon safflower/sunflower oil

⅓ cup/50 g cashew nuts

2 large red chiles, sliced (and deseeded if you prefer it mild)

1 lemongrass stalk (outer layer discarded), finely minced

2 kaffir lime leaves, shredded

1 inch/2.5 cm piece fresh ginger, unpeeled and sliced

2 garlic cloves, peeled and crushed

9 oz./250 g silken tofu, cubed

9 oz./250 g medium asparagus tips

2 red bell peppers, cut into strips

1 tablespoon tamarind paste

2 tablespoons dark soy sauce

1 tablespoon clear honey

steamed rice or egg noodles, to serve

serves 4

Heat the oil in a wok or a large skillet over medium/low heat and add the cashew nuts, chiles, lemongrass, lime leaves, ginger, and garlic. Gently sauté for 1 minute.

Add the tofu, asparagus, and red bell peppers and stir-fry for a further 2 minutes until they start to soften around the edges and the cashew nuts turn golden.

Pour in the tamarind paste, soy sauce, and honey, along with ⅓ cup/100 ml water and turn up the heat to bring the liquid to a boil. Allow the contents of the wok to bubble up so that the liquid finishes cooking the vegetables and they are lovely and tender. This should take a further 3 minutes or so.

Transfer to bowls. Remove the slices of ginger, unless you particularly like hits of feisty ginger! Serve piping hot with steamed rice or egg noodles.

Halloumi is a firm Greek cheese that is delicious eaten when hot and melting. It has a reasonably long shelf-life before it is opened, which means you can keep a pack tucked away in the fridge. Harissa is a fiery chile paste used in North African cooking—add more if you like your food spicy.

harissa-spiced chickpeas with halloumi & spinach

1 tablespoon olive oil

1 onion, finely chopped

1 garlic clove, crushed

1 tablespoon harissa paste*

14-oz./400-g can chickpeas, drained

14-oz./400-g can chopped tomatoes (flavored with garlic or mixed herbs, if available)

4½ oz./125 g halloumi cheese, cut into cubes

3½ oz./100 g baby spinach leaves

freshly squeezed juice of ½ lemon

sea salt and freshly ground black pepper

freshly grated Parmesan cheese, to serve

crisp green salad, to serve

serves 2

Pour the oil into a large pan and gently sauté the onion and garlic until softened. Add the harissa paste, chickpeas, and chopped tomatoes. Bring to a boil and let simmer for about 5 minutes.

Add the halloumi cheese and spinach, cover, and cook over a low heat for a further 5 minutes. Season to taste and stir in the lemon juice. Spoon onto serving plates and sprinkle with the Parmesan cheese. Serve immediately with a crisp green side salad.

Variation

Substitute a 14-oz./400-g can of any beans (such as borlotti, kidney, or cannellini) for the chickpeas.

*Note If you don't have harissa paste, you can make your own by mixing together ½ teaspoon cayenne pepper, 1 tablespoon ground cumin, 1 tablespoon tomato paste/purée, and the freshly squeezed juice of 1 lime.

Dill is quite a floral, grassy herb and a whiff of it conjures up springtime, which is possibly why it is so well complemented by the beans and peas in this dish. Marinating the feta first for just a few minutes lifts it from a salty, creamy cheese to something much more complex, so it's well worth it.

couscous with feta, dill, & spring beans

1¾ cups/275 g couscous

1⅔ cups/400 ml boiling water

5 tablespoons extra virgin olive oil

1 garlic clove, crushed

3 shallots, thinly sliced

2 tablespoons chopped fresh dill

2 tablespoons chopped fresh chives

1 tablespoon finely chopped preserved lemon, or 1 tablespoon zest and flesh of fresh lemon, finely chopped

9 oz./250 g feta cheese, chopped

5½ oz./150 g sugar snap peas

5½ oz./150 g frozen baby fava/broad beans, defrosted

5½ oz./150 g frozen peas, defrosted

freshly ground black pepper

serves 4

Put the couscous in a large bowl and pour over the boiling water. Cover with plastic wrap/clingfilm or a plate and leave to swell for 10 minutes.

Pour the olive oil into a mixing bowl and add the garlic, shallots, dill, chives, preserved lemon, and lots of freshly ground black pepper—the coarser the better. Add the feta, turn in the oil, and set aside while you cook the beans.

Bring a medium saucepan of unsalted water to a boil. Add the sugar snap peas, bring back to a boil, and cook for 1 minute. Add the fava/broad beans, bring back to a boil and cook for 1 minute. Finally, add the peas and cook for 2 minutes. Drain.

Uncover the couscous, stir in the hot beans, transfer to bowls and top with the feta, spooning over the flavoured oil as you go. Stir well before serving.

special occasions

The idea of making your own pastry can be a little daunting but this pastry recipe is so unintimidating that you should give it a go. It has just three ingredients and no rolling! Make the pastry in the food processor, form it into a ball, then press it directly into the tart tin. The whole tart can be made well in advance and served at room temperature with a peppery wild arugula salad.

soft goat cheese & fennel tart

4 fennel bulbs, with feathery tops intact

2 tablespoons olive oil

7 oz./200 g soft goat cheese, roughly crumbled

½ cup/65 g walnut halves

3 eggs

¾ cup/185 ml light/single cream

1 tablespoon snipped fresh chives

sea salt and freshly ground black pepper

dressed arugula/rocket leaves, to serve

tart pastry

1⅓ cups/170 g all-purpose/plain flour

6 tablespoons/80 g butter, cut into cubes and chilled

2–3 tablespoons chilled water

a loose-bottomed tart tin, about 10 inches/25 cm diameter, lightly greased

baking weights (optional)

serves 6–8

Preheat the oven to 350°F (180°C) Gas 4.

To make the pastry dough, put the flour in a food processor. With the motor running, add the butter and process until the mixture resembles coarse bread crumbs. Add the chilled water and process until the dough just starts to come together. Tip the dough out onto a lightly-floured work surface and use your hands to form it into a ball, gathering all the smaller pieces together. Do not knead it too much.

Put the dough in the centre of the prepared tart pan and use your thumbs to press it down into the pan, working outwards from the centre and making sure the pastry comes up over the side of the pan. Prick the base all over with the tines of a fork. Cover the pastry with a sheet of baking parchment and fill with baking weights, rice, or dried beans. Bake in the preheated oven for about 20 minutes, until the pastry looks dry and golden. Remove the pastry from the oven but leave the oven on.

Remove the feathery tops from the fennel. Chop them finely to give about 3 tablespoons and set aside. Cut the fennel bulbs into thin wedges. Put them in a roasting pan, add the olive oil, and season well with salt and pepper. Cook in the still-hot oven for 40 minutes, turning after 20 minutes, until golden and tender. Leave in the pan and set aside to cool to room temperature.

Arrange the fennel in the tart shell and scatter the cheese and walnuts randomly over and in between the pieces of fennel. Put the eggs, cream, and chives in a pitcher/jug or bowl. Whisk with a fork to combine, season well, and pour over the fennel. Bake in the still-hot oven for about 45 minutes, until puffed and golden on top. Serve warm or at room temperature with dressed arugula/rocket on the side.

For these savory pastries you can leave the spices whole so that the full experience can be enjoyed. The sweetness of the dried fruit cuts through the saltiness of the cheese and diffuses the heat from the chile. They are good hot or cold as part of a gourmet picnic. Or try them served with spinach, wilted with a pinch of nutmeg and the grated zest of 2 lemons, together with a bowl of yogurt spiced with toasted chile, turmeric, and cumin.

7 oz./200 g phyllo/filo pastry

2 tablespoons butter, melted

package filling

10½ oz./300 g tomatoes

1 tablespoon olive oil

1 teaspoon coriander seeds

1 teaspoon cumin seeds

1 garlic clove, crushed

½ red chile, seeded and finely chopped

1 cup/200 g couscous

⅓ cup/100 g dried chickpeas, soaked in water overnight, drained and cooked for 1–1½ hours

2½ oz./70 g dried apricots, soaked in water overnight, drained and sliced

⅓ cup/70 g raisins, soaked in water overnight, and drained

¾ cup/70 g flaked almonds, lightly toasted in a dry skillet

a handful of flat leaf parsley, finely chopped

a handful of fresh mint leaves, finely chopped

7 oz./200 g feta cheese, cubed

freshly squeezed juice of 1 lemon

sea salt and freshly ground black pepper

red onion, tomato, & olive chutney

1 red onion, finely chopped

14 oz./400 g tomatoes, quartered

1 tablespoon olive oil

½ cup/100 g pitted black olives, finely chopped

sea salt and freshly ground black pepper

2 baking sheets

serves 4

feta & chickpea parcels with onion & tomato chutney

Preheat the oven to 400°F (200°C) Gas 6.

To make the filling for the pastries, mix the tomatoes with the olive oil, spices, garlic, and chile. Season with salt, then transfer to a baking sheet. Roast in the preheated oven for 20 minutes until they collapse in on themselves.

Meanwhile, put the couscous in a bowl, add 1⅔ cups/400 ml cold water, and let soak for 10 minutes. Fluff up with a fork, then transfer to a large bowl with the chickpeas, apricots, raisins, almonds, herbs, feta, lemon juice, salt, and pepper. Stir in the roasted tomatoes and mix well.

To prepare the chutney, put the red onion and tomatoes on a baking sheet, sprinkle with olive oil, then roast at 400°F (200°C) Gas 6 for 20 minutes until tender. Transfer to a bowl and stir in the olives, mixing thoroughly. Add salt and pepper to taste.

Reduce the oven to 350°F (180°C) Gas 4. Put 3 sheets of the pastry on a work surface, overlaying them so that they form a star shape, and brush each sheet lightly with the melted butter. (Keep the rest of the pastry covered with a damp cloth to prevent it drying out.)

Divide the filling into 4 portions and put 1 portion in the middle of the top sheet of phyllo/filo, then pull up all the sides, twisting and pinching so that the filling is encased and the pastry is sealed. Repeat to make 4 generously sized parcels. Bake for 20 minutes until lightly golden, then cover with foil and cook for a further 15 minutes.

Serve the parcels with the chutney beside, and perhaps some wilted lemon spinach and spicy yogurt (see recipe introduction).

Truffled Egg Linguine sounds very impressive but is surprisingly simple—though it does call for the finest quality ingredients. As well as being fancy, this is great fun—toss it in front of your guests for a bit of restaurant-style cabaret at home. Alternatively, try the "Naked Ravioli", so called as they are missing the pasta wrapping that usually encloses the filling. They look rather chic, but actually require just a few simple ingredients.

truffled egg linguine

½ cup/125 ml light/single cream

1 tablespoon butter

2 tablespoons olive oil

4 very fresh organic eggs

10½ oz./300 g fresh linguine

1 teaspoon truffle oil

1¾ oz./50 g pecorino cheese, finely grated

2 oz./50 g Parmesan cheese, finely grated

sea salt

serves 4

Bring a large saucepan of lightly salted water to a boil.

Put the cream and butter in a small saucepan and set over low heat.

Put the olive oil in a large, non-stick skillet set over medium heat. Gently crack one egg at a time into the pan. Alternatively, to help prevent the yolks from breaking, crack each one into a small pitcher/jug, then pour into the skillet. Cook the eggs so that the whites just start to turn and firm up around the edge, then slide onto a plate.

Cook the pasta in the boiling water for 2–3 minutes, until it rises to the top—fresh pasta cooks much faster than dried. Working quickly, as you want the pasta to be as hot as possible, drain well and return to the warm pan. Pour in the cream mixture. Gently toss to combine, then divide the pasta between 4 serving plates. Put an egg on top of each one and drizzle truffle oil over each egg. Sprinkle a quarter of the cheeses over each one.

Use a spoon and fork to toss all the ingredients together so that the yolk combines with the hot pasta and thickens the sauce, and the egg whites are roughly chopped and combined with the linguine. Serve immediately.

naked spinach & ricotta ravioli with sage cream

2¼ lbs./1 kg fresh spinach, washed and roughly chopped

9 oz./250 g ricotta

5 egg yolks

4½ oz./125 g Parmesan cheese, finely grated, plus extra to serve

1 cup/125 g all-purpose/plain flour

1 tablespoon butter

12 fresh sage leaves

1 cup/250 ml light/single cream

sea salt and freshly ground black pepper

a baking sheet lined with baking parchment

serves 3–4

Bring a large saucepan of water to a boil. Add the spinach and cook for 5 minutes, until wilted and tender. Rinse with cold water and drain well. Tip the cooked spinach into the centre of a clean dish towel (use an old, threadbare one, rather than your best). Roll the dish towel up to form a log and twist the ends away from each other to squeeze out as much liquid as possible. Put the spinach on a chopping board and chop finely. Transfer to a large bowl. Add the ricotta, egg yolks, and half of the Parmesan and season with salt and pepper. Mix well to thoroughly combine.

Put the flour on a large plate. Using slightly wet hands, roll the spinach mixture into 12 walnut-sized balls. Roll each ball in flour and put them on the prepared baking sheet.

Put the butter and sage in a small saucepan and set over medium heat. Cook until the sage leaves just sizzle. Add the cream and the remaining Parmesan and cook for about 10 minutes, until thickened, stirring often to prevent the cream from catching. Bring a large saucepan of lightly salted water to a boil. Carefully drop the balls into the boiling water and cook for just 1 minute, until they rise to the surface. Drain well and arrange 4 balls in each serving dish. Spoon over the warm sage cream, sprinkle with the extra Parmesan, and grind over plenty of black pepper.

Here are two superb risottos, perfect for special occasions or entertaining, which both feel a little decadent. Wild mushrooms are an exotic treat, available at farmers' markets. Or if there is an occasion where you have a glass of Champagne left over, try using it in this light and summery risotto. Conversely, open a bottle just to use what you need for this recipe and drink the remainder while you are stirring the risotto!

Champagne risotto with lemon thyme tomatoes

foraged mushroom risotto

1 oz./25 g dried porcini mushrooms

4 cups/1 litre vegetable stock

½ cup/125 ml dry white wine

2 tablespoons olive oil

3 tablespoons butter

1 lb 2 oz./500 g mixed foraged or wild mushrooms, roughly chopped

1 onion, chopped

2 garlic cloves, finely chopped

1⅔ cups/330 g arborio (risotto) rice

3½ oz./100 g Parmesan cheese, finely grated

a small handful of fresh flat leaf parsley, finely chopped

sea salt and freshly ground black pepper

serves 4

Put the dried mushrooms in a heatproof bowl and pour in 2 cups/500 ml boiling water. Let soak for 30 minutes, then drain, reserving 1 cup/250 ml of the liquid. Finely chop the mushrooms and set aside. Put the reserved mushroom liquid in a saucepan. Add the stock and wine and set over low heat.

Heat 1 tablespoon of the oil and half of the butter in a heavy-based saucepan set over medium heat. Add the fresh mushrooms and cook for 8–10 minutes, until soft and aromatic. Remove from the pan and set aside.

Add the remaining oil and butter to the mushroom pan. Add the onion and garlic and cook for 2–3 minutes, until softened. Add the rice and stir for 1 minute, until the rice is glossy. Reduce the heat to low, add about ½ cup/125 ml of the hot stock mixture and cook, stirring often, until the stock has been absorbed. Repeat until all the stock has been used and the rice is tender yet still firm to the bite. Stir in half of the Parmesan, season, and serve with the remaining Parmesan and parsley sprinkled over the top.

4 cups/1 litre vegetable stock

1 cup/250 ml Champagne or other sparkling white wine, such as cava or prosecco

3 tablespoons butter

1 leek, thinly sliced

1 garlic clove, finely chopped

1½ cups/330 g arborio (risotto) rice

2 oz./50 g Parmesan cheese, finely grated

1 tablespoon light olive oil

16–20 small yellow tomatoes

2 sprigs fresh lemon thyme

sea salt and freshly ground black pepper

Parmesan shavings, to serve

serves 4

Put the stock and Champagne in a saucepan over medium heat and gently simmer.

Set a heavy-based saucepan over medium heat and add 2 tablespoons of the butter. When the butter is sizzling, add the leek and garlic to the pan and cook for 4–5 minutes, until the leek has softened but not browned. Add the rice and cook for 1 minute, stirring well. Add a small ladle of the hot stock mixture to the pan and stir for a few minutes, until almost all the stock has been absorbed. Repeat until all the stock has been added and the rice is soft but still firm to the bite, adding a little extra water if necessary. Stir in the remaining butter and the Parmesan and cover the pan until needed.

Put the olive oil in a skillet over medium heat. Add the tomatoes, thyme sprigs, sea salt, and black pepper and cook for 3–4 minutes, shaking the skillet, until the tomatoes have softened and are just starting to split.

Serve the risotto in bowls with the tomatoes on top and offer Parmesan shavings on the side for sprinkling.

This is a vegetarian take on the classic Spanish rice dish paella. It's colorful, delicious, bursting with fresh, young vegetables, and enhanced with the subtle flavor of saffron and rosemary. Perfect for summer entertaining.

paella of summer vine vegetables with almonds

a large pinch of saffron threads

⅓ cup/80 ml olive oil

7 oz./200 g red or yellow cherry tomatoes

3½ oz./100 g green beans

4 baby zucchini/courgettes, halved

3 oz./85 g freshly shelled peas

2 garlic cloves, chopped

2 fresh rosemary sprigs

1½ cups/320 g arborio (risotto) rice

3⅓ cups/800 ml vegetable stock

½ cup/30 g slivered/flaked almonds, lightly toasted

serves 4

Put the saffron in a bowl with ⅓ cup/65 ml hot water and set aside to infuse. Heat half of the oil in a heavy-based skillet set over high heat and add the tomatoes. Cook for 2 minutes, shaking the skillet so that the tomatoes soften and start to split. Use a slotted spoon to remove the tomatoes from the skillet and set aside. Add the beans, zucchini/courgettes, and peas and stir-fry over high heat for 2–3 minutes. Set aside with the tomatoes until needed.

Add the remaining oil to the skillet with the garlic and rosemary, and cook gently for 1 minute to flavor the oil. Add the rice to the skillet and cook, stirring constantly, for 2 minutes, until the rice is shiny and opaque. Add the stock and saffron water to the skillet. Stir just once or twice, then increase the heat. When the stock is rapidly boiling and little holes have formed in the rice, reduce the heat to medium and let simmer gently for about 20 minutes, until almost all the stock has been absorbed.

Scatter the cooked tomatoes, beans, zucchini/courgettes, and peas over the rice, cover lightly with some foil, and cook over low heat for 5 minutes so that the vegetables are just heated through. Sprinkle the almonds on top to serve.

You need to be careful when buying ricotta because it can sometimes be very soggy, especially when sold in tubs. The organic varieties or buffalo ricotta are crumbly rather than creamy, which is what you're after here. Buffalo mozzarella also works well, as does a soft, fresh goat cheese. Leave some seeds in the chile to give a little kick, awaken all the other flavors, and contrast with the sweet nuts.

winter-spiced salad with pears, honeyed pecans, & ricotta

1 star anise

1 cinnamon stick

2 pears, unpeeled, quartered and cored

5½ oz./150 g mixed salad greens, such as arugula/rocket, shredded radicchio or baby Swiss chard

4½ oz./125 g fresh ricotta, preferably buffalo milk ricotta

honeyed pecans

½ cup/50 g pecans

¼ teaspoon dried hot pepper/chilli flakes

¼ teaspoon fennel seeds

3 tablespoons clear honey

sea salt

dressing

4 tablespoons safflower/sunflower oil

1 tablespoon walnut oil

freshly squeezed juice of 1 lemon

1 large red chile, partly seeded and chopped

serves 4

Fill a medium saucepan with water and add the star anise and cinnamon stick. Bring to a boil and add the pears. Poach for 12 minutes, or until tender.

Put the pecans, a large pinch of salt, the dried hot pepper/chilli flakes, and the fennel seeds in a skillet and toast until golden and aromatic. Pour in the honey, turn the heat right up, and leave to bubble away for a few minutes. Tip onto baking parchment and leave to cool.

Meanwhile, to make the dressing, whisk together the safflower/sunflower and walnut oils, the lemon juice, and chile.

Transfer the salad greens to bowls, scatter over the pears, and crumble over the ricotta. Drizzle with the dressing. Roughly break up the nuts with your fingers and scatter them over the top.

family gatherings

These vibrant salads, one cold, one warm, both combine crisp summer vegetables and soft creamy cheeses, with delicious results. When making either, make sure to leave enough time for them to stand for a while before serving to let the flavors develop. Serve with slices of toasted bread.

tomato & mozzarella salad with eggplant relish

6 mixed ripe tomatoes, thinly sliced

3 large balls of fresh buffalo mozzarella, torn

eggplant relish

1 eggplant/aubergine, cut into small cubes

1 teaspoon salt

⅓ cup/85 ml light olive oil

1 red onion, finely diced

2 garlic cloves, chopped

1 celery rib/stick, finely diced

1 tablespoon small salted caperberries/capers, rinsed

1 small red bell pepper, finely diced

¾ cup/90 g small black olives

¼ cup/65 ml red wine vinegar

2 teaspoons white sugar

a handful of fresh mint leaves, finely sliced

sea salt and freshly ground black pepper

serves 4

To make the relish, put the eggplant/aubergine in a colander with the salt and use your hands to toss together. Let sit for 30 minutes, then using your hands, squeeze out as much liquid from the eggplant/aubergine as you can, without squashing the flesh too much.

Put the oil in a skillet set over high heat. Add the onion and cook for 2 minutes. Add the eggplant/aubergine and cook for 8–10 minutes, stirring often, until golden. Add the garlic and cook for 1 minute only. Add the celery, bell pepper, caperberries, and olives and stir-fry for just 1 minute so that the vegetables stay crisp. Add the vinegar and sugar to the skillet and bring to a boil, cooking for a minute. Remove from the heat and season. Let sit at room temperature for at least 30 minutes to infuse.

Arrange the tomato slices on a large serving plate and scatter the mozzarella pieces over the top. Spoon over the relish and sprinkle with the mint to serve.

chile-roasted vegetables with soft goat cheese

4 small red or yellow bell peppers, sliced

1 fennel bulb, thinly sliced and fronds chopped

8 ripe tomatoes, halved

2 garlic cloves, thinly sliced

2 large red chiles, deseeded and thinly sliced

1 teaspoon sea salt

¼ cup/65 ml olive oil

7 oz./200 g soft goat cheese, sliced

a small handful of fresh basil leaves

2 tablespoons balsamic vinegar

toasted sourdough bread, to serve

serves 4

Preheat the oven to 350°F (180°C) Gas 4.

Put the bell peppers, fennel, fennel fronds, tomatoes, garlic, and chiles in a large bowl with the salt and oil. Toss until evenly coated in the oil and arrange in a roasting pan. Roast in the preheated oven for about 1 hour, turning once after about 30 minutes, until the vegetables are just starting to char around the edges. Remove from the oven and let cool a little for about 20 minutes

Lift the still-warm vegetables onto a large serving plate, reserving the cooking juices. Top with the cheese and basil leaves. Mix the reserved juices with the vinegar and spoon over the salad. Let sit for a little while before serving at room temperature, with toasted sourdough bread for mopping up the delicious juices.

This tasty, gorgeous-looking rice dish is inspired by the salade Niçoise, the popular plate from southern France. It has generous handfuls of market-fresh herbs and the key flavors of summer-ripe tomatoes, black olives, green beans, and hard-boiled eggs.

Niçoise-style brown rice salad with fresh herbs

4 eggs

7 oz./200 g baby green beans

12 oz./350 g short-grain brown rice

¼ cup/60 ml olive oil

1 garlic clove, crushed

2 tablespoons freshly squeezed lemon juice

7 oz./200 g cherry tomatoes, halved

½ cup/60 g black olives, pitted and halved

1 small of bunch fresh chives, finely snipped

1 large handful of fresh parsley, chopped

1 large handful of fresh basil leaves

1 large handful of fresh mint leaves

1 small handful of fresh tarragon leaves

sea salt and freshly ground black pepper

serves 4

Put the eggs in a small saucepan and cover with cold water. Set over high heat and bring to a boil. Cook for 3 minutes, then rinse under cold water. When cool enough to handle, peel and halve them then set aside.

Cook the beans in boiling water for 1 minute. Drain and put in a bowl of cold water. Put the rice in a sieve and rinse well under cold running water. Transfer the rice to a large saucepan and cover with just-boiled water. Set the pan over high heat, return the water to a boil, and cook the rice for 10–12 minutes until it is tender but retains some "bite". Tip the rice into a sieve, rinse under cold running water, and drain well.

Put the rice and drained beans in a large bowl and add the oil, garlic, and lemon juice. Stir until the rice is coated in the oil. Add the tomatoes, olives, and herbs, toss to combine, and season to taste with salt and pepper. Arrange the egg halves on top to serve.

Two international dishes to please: the vibrant colors of Kerala, India's southern-most state, are all here on a plate in this deliciously creamy curry. The term Napolitana is used loosely here to describe the predominance of tomatoes in this Mediterranean-style stew, although the flavors could easily be described as Greek, given the inclusion of fresh oregano and feta cheese.

creamy vegetable & cashew curry

2 tablespoons vegetable oil

4½ oz./125 g large, unsalted cashews

6 shallots, peeled and halved

1 teaspoon black mustard seeds

6–8 curry leaves

2 garlic cloves, chopped

1 tablespoon finely grated fresh ginger

1 teaspoon turmeric

4 large dried red chiles

1 small red bell pepper, thinly sliced

2 ripe tomatoes, quartered

8 very small new potatoes, halved

14-oz./400-ml can coconut milk

steamed or boiled basmati rice, to serve (optional)

serves 4

Put the oil in a heavy-based saucepan set over medium heat. Add the cashews and shallots and cook for 5 minutes, stirring often, until the cashew are just starting to brown. Add the mustard seeds and curry leaves and cook until the seeds start to pop. Add the garlic, ginger, turmeric, chiles, and red bell pepper to the pan and stir-fry for 2 minutes, until aromatic.

Add the tomatoes, potatoes, and coconut milk, partially cover the pan, and let simmer gently over low heat for about 20 minutes, or until the potatoes are cooked through. Spoon over basmati rice to serve, if liked.

Napolitana lentil stew

½ cup/100 g green or brown lentils

3 tablespoons olive oil

1 onion, chopped

2 garlic cloves, chopped

a small handful of fresh oregano, chopped

1 teaspoon dried hot pepper/chilli flakes

1½ tablespoons salted caperberries/capers, rinsed

2 ripe tomatoes, roughly chopped

1 cup/250 ml tomato purée/passata

½ cup/60 g small black olives

3½ oz./100 g feta cheese, crumbled

crusty bread, to serve

serves 4

Put the lentils in a large saucepan, add sufficient cold water to cover, and set over high heat. Bring to a boil, then reduce the heat and let simmer for 20 minutes until the lentils are tender but retain a little "bite". Drain and set aside until needed.

Put the oil in a saucepan set over high heat. Add the onion, garlic, oregano, and dried hot pepper/chilli flakes and cook for 5 minutes, stirring often, until the onion softens. Add the caperberries/capers, tomatoes, tomato purée/passata, lentils, and 1 cup/250 ml water. Bring to a boil, then reduce the heat and let simmer gently for 10 minutes, stirring occasionally.

Spoon into warmed serving dishes, top with the olives and crumbled feta, and serve with crusty bread on the side for dipping into the rich sauce.

So many iconic international meat-free dishes are based on eggplant, such as the spicy Middle Eastern dip baba ghanoush, Sicilian caponata and the French classic ratatouille. Here it forms the basis of this wonderfully colorful stew. Spiced Potatoes—a dish from Mumbai—make a great side for the curry, or it can be served with basmati rice.

eggplant, tomato & red lentil curry

3 tablespoons light olive oil

1 large eggplant/aubergine, cut into 8 pieces

1 red onion, chopped

2 garlic cloves, chopped

1 tablespoon finely chopped fresh ginger

9 oz./250 g cherry tomatoes on the vine

6–8 curry leaves

1 teaspoon ground cumin

¼ teaspoon chili powder

1 tablespoon tomato paste/purée

⅔ cup/125 g red split lentils

1 handful of fresh cilantro/coriander, roughly chopped

basmati rice or spiced potatoes, to serve (optional)

serves 4

Heat 2 tablespoons of oil in a skillet set over high heat. When the oil is smoking hot add the eggplant/aubergine to the skillet and cook for 5 minutes, turning the pieces often so that they cook evenly. At first it will absorb the oil, but as it cooks to a dark and golden color, the oil will start to seep out back into the skillet. Remove the eggplant/aubergine from the skillet at this point.

Add the remaining oil, onion, garlic, and ginger to the skillet and cook for 5 minutes. Add the cherry tomatoes and cook for 1 minute, until they just soften and collapse, then remove them from the skillet before they break up too much and set aside.

Add the curry leaves and cumin to the skillet and cook for a couple of minutes as the curry leaves pop and crackle. Add the chili powder, tomato paste/purée, 2 cups/480 ml water, and the lentils and simmer for 15–20 minutes, until the lentils are tender but retain some "bite". Stir in the eggplant/aubergine and cherry tomatoes and cook the curry for a couple of minutes just to warm through. Stir in the cilantro/coriander and serve with basmati rice or Spiced Potatoes (opposite).

spiced potatoes

1 lb./500 g potatoes, peeled and cubed

4 tablespoons safflower/sunflower oil

2 teaspoons black mustard seeds

1 teaspoon medium or hot chili powder, or paprika

4 teaspoons cumin seeds

8–10 fresh curry leaves

2 teaspoons ground coriander

2 teaspoons ground cumin

1 teaspoon ground turmeric

6 tablespoons freshly chopped cilantro/coriander leaves

freshly squeezed lemon juice, to taste

salt and freshly ground black pepper

serves 4

Cook the potatoes in a pan of salted boiling water until tender.

Heat the safflower/sunflower oil in a large, non-stick wok or skillet. Add the mustard seeds, chili powder, cumin seeds, and curry leaves. Stir-fry for 1–2 minutes, then add the ground coriander, cumin, turmeric, and potatoes. Season well and stir-fry over high heat for 4–5 minutes.

Stir in the fresh cilantro/coriander and lemon juice, to taste, and serve.

Fresh chestnuts aren't always easy to find, but if you can get your hands on some, then use them to make this delicious pasta dish which has a slightly festive flavor. Don't feel too guilty about the cream—the chestnuts are low in both fat and calories.

pappardelle pasta with portobello mushrooms & chestnuts

7 oz./200 g fresh chestnuts

1 tablespoon olive oil

1 tablespoon butter

2 garlic cloves, chopped

14 oz./400 g portobello or field mushrooms, sliced

2 fresh thyme sprigs

½ cup/125 ml dry white wine

1 cup/250 ml light/single cream

1 bunch of chives, cut into 1-inch/2.5-cm lengths

2 oz./50 g pecorino cheese, finely grated, plus extra to serve

14 oz./400 g pappardelle, tagliatelle or any other ribbon pasta

sea salt and freshly ground black pepper

serves 4

Preheat the oven to 400ºF (200ºC) Gas 6.

Score a cross on one end of each chestnut. Put them on a baking sheet and roast in the preheated oven for 10–15 minutes, until the skins split. Remove and let cool. When cool enough to handle, pull off the shells and rub away the fleshy skin underneath. Set aside until needed.

Put the oil and butter in a skillet set over high heat. When the butter sizzles, add the garlic and cook for just 1 minute, making sure it doesn't burn. Add the mushrooms and thyme, reduce the heat to medium, and partially cover with a lid. Cook for 10 minutes, stirring often. Add the wine to the skillet and simmer until the liquid is reduced by half. Add the cream, reduce the heat, and cook for 15 minutes, until the mixture thickens. Add the chives and pecorino and stir to combine. Season to taste with salt and pepper. Cover with foil to keep warm.

Cook the pasta according to the packet instructions. Drain well and return to the warm pan. Add the mushroom sauce, gently toss to mix, and serve immediately with extra pecorino cheese for sprinkling.

These spicy and satisfying Moroccan recipes are perfect vegetarian food for sharing, either served on their own or as part of a hot buffet. Couscous is an excellent choice when cooking for a larger number of people, too, since it doesn't need cooking—it is simply soaked in vegetable stock and fluffed up with a fork.

Moroccan-style roasted vegetable couscous

2 small red onions
1 sweet potato
2 red bell peppers
2 small leeks
2 garlic cloves, halved
2 tablespoons olive oil
½ teaspoon dried hot red pepper/chilli flakes
1 cup/150 g couscous
1¼ cups/300 ml hot vegetable stock or water

a handful of fresh mint sprigs
freshly squeezed lemon juice, to taste
sea salt and freshly ground black pepper

a non-stick baking sheet or small roasting pan

serves 4

Preheat the oven to 400°F (200°C) Gas 6.

Remove the skin from the onions and slice them into thin wedges. Peel the sweet potato and cut it into chunks. Core and deseed the peppers, then cut into thick slices. Trim the leeks, then split them and wash them well. Dry with paper towels, and cut into large chunks.

Put the prepared vegetables and garlic on a nonstick baking sheet or in a small roasting pan. Pour the olive oil over the top, add the dried hot pepper/chilli flakes, and use your hands to toss the vegetables until they are coated with the oil mixture. Place the pan in the preheated oven and cook for about 20–25 minutes, until the vegetables are tender.

Meanwhile, put the couscous in a large heatproof bowl and pour over the hot vegetable stock. Cover and set aside until the couscous swells and absorbs all the liquid, about 10 minutes.

Use a fork to fluff up the couscous, then add the roasted vegetables and mint. Add a little lemon juice and season to taste with salt and pepper. Serve whilst still warm.

spicy carrot & chickpea tagine with honey

3–4 tablespoons olive oil
1 onion, finely chopped
3–4 garlic cloves, finely chopped
2 teaspoons ground turmeric
1–2 teaspoons cumin seeds
1 teaspoon ground cinnamon
½ teaspoon cayenne pepper
½ teaspoon ground black pepper
1 tablespoon clear honey

3–4 medium carrots, sliced on the diagonal
2 x 14-oz./400-g. cans of chickpeas, thoroughly rinsed and drained
sea salt
1–2 tablespoons rosewater
a bunch of fresh cilantro/coriander leaves, finely chopped
1 lemon, cut into wedges, to serve
plain yogurt, to serve

serves 4

Heat the oil in a heavy-based, flameproof casserole dish. Add the onion and garlic, and sauté until soft. Add the turmeric, cumin, cinnamon, cayenne, black pepper, honey, and carrots. Pour in enough water to cover the base of the dish and cover with a lid. Cook gently for 10–15 minutes.

Toss in the chickpeas, check that there is still enough liquid at the base of the dish, cover with the lid, and cook gently for a further 5–10 minutes. Season with salt, sprinkle the rosewater and cilantro/coriander leaves over the top, and serve with lemon wedges for squeezing and yogurt for spooning.

This is a hearty hotpot packed with fall vegetables and rich with smoky paprika. Great northern beans are large and white with a distinctive, delicate flavor. If you can't find them, lima/butter beans will do just as well. The Upside-down Bell Pepper & Tomato Pie makes a great accompaniment to the hotpot, or is equally tasty served as a brunch dish for sharing.

smoky hotpot of great northern beans

½ cup/100 g dried great northern or lima/butter beans

2 tablespoons olive oil

1 large onion, chopped

2 garlic cloves, chopped

1 handful of fresh flat leaf parsley, chopped

2 teaspoons smoked Spanish paprika (pimentón)

1 celery rib/stick, chopped

1 carrot, chopped

2 medium waxy potatoes, cut into 1-inch/2.5-cm dice

1 red bell pepper, chopped

2 cups/500 ml vegetable stock

sea salt and freshly ground black pepper

crusty bread, to serve

serves 6

Soak the dried beans in cold water for at least 6 hours or ideally overnight. Drain and put in a saucepan with sufficient just-boiled water to cover. Cook for 30 minutes until softened. Drain and set aside until needed.

Put the oil in a saucepan set over medium heat. Add the onion and cook for 4–5 minutes until softened. Add the garlic, parsley, and paprika to the pan and stir-fry for 2 minutes. Add the celery, carrot, potatoes, and red bell pepper and cook for 2 minutes, stirring constantly to coat the vegetables in the flavoured oil. Add the stock and beans and bring to a boil. Reduce the heat and partially cover the pan with a lid. Let simmer for 40 minutes, stirring often, until all the vegetables are cooked. Season to taste and serve with crusty bread for dipping in the sauce.

upside-down bell pepper & tomato pie

2 tablespoons olive oil

1 small red bell pepper, sliced

2 small red onions, quartered

2 garlic cloves, chopped

14-oz./400-g can chopped tomatoes

sea salt and freshly ground black pepper

pastry

2 cups/250 g all-purpose/plain flour

2 teaspoons baking powder

5½ oz./150 g Cheddar cheese, grated

1 teaspoon sea salt

3 tablespoons butter, melted

2 eggs, lightly beaten

¼ cup/65 ml buttermilk

a large, non-stick skillet with a oven-proof handle

serves 6

To make the pastry, put the flour, baking powder, cheese, and salt in the bowl of a food processor. Pulse a couple of times just to combine. Put the melted butter, eggs, and buttermilk in a pitcher/jug and whisk to combine. With the motor of the food processor running, slowly add the egg mixture until the dough becomes sticky. Let sit for 30 minutes while you make the topping.

Preheat the oven to 350°F (180°C) Gas 4. Put the oil in a skillet and set over high heat. Add the bell pepper, onions, and garlic and cook for 10 minutes, until the pepper slices start to turn golden. Add the tomatoes, season, and cook for 5 minutes, until almost all the liquid has evaporated. Leave the mixture in the skillet and set aside to cool.

Tip the dough onto a floured sheet of baking parchment and form it into a circle the same size as the skillet. Slide the dough onto the tomato mixture in the skillet. Cook in the preheated oven for 20–25 minutes, until the pastry has risen and is golden. Let cool for a few minutes and turn out onto a serving plate. Cut into slices and serve warm.

This rich risotto is made from sweet pumpkin and creamy Gorgonzola. The pumkin retains its deep flavor and unique texture here as it's roasted separately, then added to a basic risotto. Or you could try another warming, comforting dish—a well-loved potato gratin. Serve on its own with a mixed green salad, or as part of a vegetable selection.

pumpkin & Gorgonzola risotto

1 lb./500 g peeled and cubed pumpkin

1 tablespoon light olive oil

4 cups/1 litre vegetable stock

2 tablespoons butter

1 leek, halved lengthwise and thinly sliced

1 garlic clove, chopped

1½ cups/330 g arborio (risotto) rice

2 oz./50 g Gorgonzola cheese, crumbled

serves 4

Preheat the oven to 350°F (180°C) Gas 4.

Put the pumpkin on a baking sheet, drizzle with the olive oil, and roast in the preheated oven for 30 minutes.

Put the stock in a saucepan and heat until gently simmering. Melt the butter in a second saucepan over high heat and add the leek and garlic. Cook for 4–5 minutes, stirring often, until the leeks have softened but not browned.

Add the rice to the leeks and stir for 1 minute, until the rice is well coated with oil. Add ½ cup/125 ml of the hot stock to the rice and cook, stirring constantly, until the rice has absorbed most of the liquid. Repeat this process until all the stock has been used, this will take about 20–25 minutes. The rice should be soft but still have a slight "bite" to the centre.

Add the roasted pumpkin pieces. Remove the pan from the heat, stir in the Gorgonzola, and serve immediately.

creamy potato gratin

4½ lb./2 kg waxy salad-style potatoes, cut in half if large

8 cups/2 litres whole milk

1 fresh bay leaf

2 tablespoons unsalted butter

2¼ cups/550 ml whipping cream

a pinch of grated nutmeg

coarse sea salt

a baking dish, 12 inch/30 cm long

serves 4–6

Preheat the oven to 350°F (180°C) Gas 4

Put the potatoes in a large saucepan with the milk and bay leaf. Bring to a boil, then lower the heat, add a pinch of salt and simmer gently until part-cooked, about 5–10 minutes.

Drain the potatoes. When cool enough to handle (but still hot), slice into rounds about ⅛ inch/3 mm thick.

Spread the butter in the bottom of the baking dish. Arrange half the potato slices in the dish and sprinkle with salt. Put the remaining potato on top and sprinkle with more salt. Pour in the cream and sprinkle with the grated nutmeg.

Bake in the preheated oven until golden and the cream is almost absorbed, but not completely, about 45 minutes. Serve hot.

Dark soy sauce, sweet mirin and dry sake make up the unique flavors of teriyaki. Add fresh or dried shiitake mushrooms to the marinade for a richer flavor. Marinating the tofu in this assertive Japanese sauce also gives it a succulent, delicate character. You can buy ready-made teriyaki sauce, but it only faintly resembles the real thing, so try to make your own—it's very easy and well worth it.

roasted teriyaki tofu steaks with glazed green vegetables

1 lb./500 g fresh firm tofu, cut into 4 pieces

4 fresh or dried shiitake mushrooms (optional)

7 oz./200 g fresh or dried egg noodles

teriyaki marinade

½ cup/125 ml dark soy sauce

½ cup/125 ml mirin (Japanese sweet rice wine)

½ cup/125 ml sake

1 tablespoon sugar

glazed green vegetables

2 tablespoons safflower/sunflower oil

2 garlic cloves, finely sliced

7 oz./200 g broccoli florets or young purple sprouting broccoli, chopped

1 leek, white and light green parts finely sliced

7 oz./200 g baby bok choy/pak choi, quartered lengthwise, or spinach, chopped

1 fennel bulb, trimmed and finely sliced

2 teaspoons cornstarch/cornflour mixed with 4 tablespoons cold water

2 scallions/spring onions, finely sliced diagonally, to serve

1 tablespoon sesame seeds, pan-toasted, to serve

serves 4

Preheat the oven to 425°F (220°C) Gas 7

To make the marinade, put the soy sauce, mirin, sake, and sugar in a large skillet and heat, stirring until the sugar has dissolved. Add the tofu and mushrooms, if using. Simmer gently for about 15 minutes, turning the tofu over halfway through cooking.

Transfer the tofu steaks to a lightly oiled baking dish or roasting pan. Spoon a little sauce on top and roast in the preheated oven for 10 minutes. Keep them warm. Using a slotted spoon, remove the mushrooms from the remaining sauce, squeeze dry, and slice finely. Reserve the sauce.

To make the glazed vegetables, heat a wok until hot, then add the oil. Add the garlic, broccoli, leek, and sliced mushrooms and stir-fry for 2 minutes. Add the bok choy/pak choi or spinach and fennel. Stir-fry for 2 minutes. Add the reserved sauce and ¼ cup/75 ml water, stir, cover, and cook for 2 minutes. Push the vegetables to the back of the wok, add the cornstarch/cornflour mixture to the bubbling juices and stir until thickened. Mix the vegetables into the sauce. Cook the noodles according to the packet instructions, then drain.

To serve, put a nest of noodles on warmed plates and pile on the vegetables. Turn the tofu steaks over and put shiny side up on top of the vegetables. Sprinkle with scallions/spring onions and toasted sesame seeds, and serve.

easy entertaining

There are so many beautifully colored tomato and bell pepper varieties now it's easy to make a really spectacular looking tart. This one makes a lovely summer lunch for friends, served with a simple green salad.

heirloom tomato, bell pepper, & mozzarella tart

13 oz./375 g sheet ready-rolled puff pastry, defrosted if frozen

1 large or two smaller red bell peppers (about 8 oz./225 g in total)

1 large or two smaller yellow peppers (about 8 oz./225 g in total)

3 tablespoons olive oil

2 garlic cloves garlic, flattened

4 heaped tablespoons red pesto, fresh or from a jar

5½ oz./150 g buffalo mozzarella, drained and finely sliced

4½ oz./125 g red cherry tomatoes, destalked and halved

4½ oz./125 g yellow cherry tomatoes, destalked and halved

½ tsp dried oregano or marjoram

1 medium egg, lightly beaten

3 tablespoons freshly grated or shaved Parmesan cheese

a few basil leaves

salt and freshly ground black pepper

a roasting pan

a rectangular baking sheet, lightly greased

serves 4

Preheat the oven to 400°F (200°C) Gas 6.

Take the pastry out of the fridge at least 20 minutes before you need to unroll it. Quarter the bell peppers, remove the pith and seeds, and cut each quarter into half lengthways. Put them in a roasting pan with the garlic cloves, pour over 2 tablespoons of the olive oil, mix together well, and roast for about 20–25 minutes until the edges of the peppers are beginning to blacken. Remove and cool for 10 minutes.

Unroll the pastry and lay on a lightly greased rectangular baking sheet. With a sharp knife score a line round the pastry about ½ inch/15 mm from the edge. Spread the pesto evenly inside the rectangle you've marked. Lay the bell pepper strips across the base of the tart, alternating red and yellow sections. Tear the mozzarella slices roughly and distribute over the peppers. Grind over some black pepper. Arrange the halved tomatoes over the peppers, red on yellow and yellow on red. Rub the oregano or marjoram over the tart, season with a little salt and a little more pepper and trickle over the remaining oil.

Turn the oven heat up to 425°F (220°C) Gas 7. Brush the edges of the tart with the beaten egg and bake for 12 minutes or until the edge of the tart is well puffed up and beginning to brown. Turn the heat back down again to 400°F (200°C) Gas 6 and cook for another 12–15 minutes until the tops of the tomatoes are well browned. Coarsely grate or shave a little Parmesan over the tart then leave to cool for 5 minutes. Tear the basil leaves roughly and scatter them over the tart. Serve warm.

Classic potato gnocchi originate in northern Italy, where they are a staple food. They are served just with melted butter and Parmesan, or maybe a tomato sauce, but they are great with pesto made from peppery arugula and sweet, creamy walnuts. They must be made with a good floury potato to give them the correct lightness: they should never be like bullets, but puffy little pillows of potato.

gnocchi with arugula pesto

2 lb./900 g floury potatoes, unpeeled

1 teaspoon salt

4 tablespoons/50 g butter, melted

1 small egg, beaten

2 cups/250 g all-purpose/plain white flour

Parmesan cheese, shaved, to serve

arugula pesto

3½ oz./100 g arugula/rocket leaves

finely grated zest of 1 unwaxed lemon

2–3 garlic cloves

½ cup/50 g shelled walnuts

¾ cup/200 ml good olive oil, plus extra to cover

2 oz./50 g Parmesan cheese, finely grated

sea salt and freshly ground black pepper

serves 4

To make the gnocchi, cook the unpeeled potatoes in boiling water for 20–30 minutes until very tender; drain well.

Meanwhile, to make the pesto, put the arugula/rocket, lemon zest, garlic, walnuts, olive oil, Parmesan, salt, and pepper in a food processor and blend until it is the texture you want. Scrape out into a jar, level the surface and pour in enough olive oil to cover.

Halve the potatoes and press through a potato ricer, or peel and press through a strainer/sieve into a bowl. While they are still warm, add 1 teaspoon salt, the butter, beaten egg, and half the flour. Mix lightly, then transfer to a floured board. Gradually knead in enough of the remaining flour to yield a smooth, soft, slightly sticky dough. Roll the dough into thick sausages, 1 inch/2.5 cm in diameter. Cut into 1 inch/2.5 cm lengths and shape into corks or pull each one down over the back of a fork to produce the traditional ridged outside and the concave inside. Put them on a lightly floured dish towel.

Bring a large saucepan of salted water to a boil. Cook the gnocchi in batches. Drop them into the boiling water and cook for 2–3 minutes or until they float to the surface. As soon as they rise, remove immediately with a slotted spoon and keep hot while you cook the remainder. Toss with the pesto and serve immediately, topped with shaved Parmesan.

Note The pesto can be stored in a jar, covered with a layer of oil, for up to 2 weeks in the refrigerator.

Lasagne may well be one of the best-loved of all Italian pasta dishes. Here, mushrooms are combined with fontina cheese and a creamy béchamel sauce, with mouthwatering results.

wild mushroom lasagne

4 tablespoons/50 g butter
2 tablespoons olive oil
1 large white onion, sliced
2 garlic cloves, chopped
2 bay leaves
2¼ lbs./1 kg wild mushrooms, sliced
1 cup/250 ml vegetable stock
1 tablespoon tomato paste/purée
13 oz./375-g fresh lasagne sheets
10½ oz./300 g fontina cheese, grated
2 oz./50 g Parmesan cheese, finely grated
sea salt and freshly ground black pepper

béchamel sauce
4 tablespoons/50 g butter
2 tablespoons all-purpose/plain flour
¼ teaspoon freshly grated nutmeg
3 cups/750 ml whole milk

serves 8

To make the béchamel sauce, put the butter in a medium saucepan set over medium heat. When the butter sizzles, stir in the flour and nutmeg and cook for 1 minute, stirring constantly. Remove from the heat and pour the milk into the pan, whisking constantly. Return the pan to low heat and cook for 5 minutes, stirring constantly, until the sauce is smooth and creamy.

Preheat the oven to 350°F (180°C) Gas 4 and oil a baking dish with half the oil. Put the butter and the remaining oil in a skillet set over high heat and add the onion, garlic, and bay leaves. Cook for 5 minutes until the onion has softened and turned translucent. Add the mushrooms, reduce the heat to medium, and cook for 15 minutes, stirring occasionally, until the mushrooms are evenly cooked. Add the stock and tomato paste/purée and increase the heat to high. Simmer rapidly until the liquid has reduced by half. Season well with salt and pepper.

Line the bottom of the oiled baking dish with lasagne sheets. Spread over a third of the sauce. Add one-third each of the mushrooms and grated fontina cheese. Repeat the process and finish with a sheet of lasagne. Spoon over the remaining sauce and sprinkle with Parmesan. Bake in the preheated oven for 45 minutes, until golden brown and bubbling. Leave to rest for 10 minutes before serving.

In the language of Provence, a "tian" is a shallow clay dish and also any dish cooked in it. Overlapping layers of vegetables are arranged in the dish, then baked in the oven. Some vegetables, such as tomatoes and zucchini, are prone to throwing off a lot of liquid, so it's a good idea to remove some beforehand by roasting or salting (rather inelegantly known as "degorging").

Provençal tian

6 large ripe tomatoes, halved

4 garlic cloves, finely sliced

6 small eggplants/aubergines, thickly sliced lengthwise

3 green or yellow zucchini/courgettes, thickly sliced lengthwise

6 tablespoons olive oil, plus extra for brushing

2 large red onions, thickly sliced

2 tablespoons chopped fresh thyme leaves

sea salt and freshly ground black pepper

topping

grated zest of 1 unwaxed lemon

3 garlic cloves, crushed

5 oz./140 g dried bread crumbs

6 tablespoons freshly grated Parmesan cheese

sprigs of basil, to serve (optional)

serves 4–6

Preheat the oven to 400°F (200°C) Gas 6

Put the tomatoes on a baking sheet, cut side up, and push slivers of garlic into each one. Roast in the preheated oven for about 30 minutes to remove some of the moisture. Remove the tomatoes from the oven and leave the oven on.

Put the sliced eggplants/aubergines and zucchini/courgettes on a plate, sprinkle with salt, and set aside for 30 minutes to extract some of the moisture. Rinse and pat dry with kitchen paper.

Heat the oil in a large skillet, add the onion, and sauté until softened and translucent. Remove from the pan and spread over the base of a tian or other shallow ceramic ovenproof dish.

Arrange overlapping layers of the eggplants/aubergines, tomatoes, and zucchini/courgettes on top—arrange them in lines across the dish, like fish scales. Tuck the chopped thyme between the layers.

Brush with the extra olive oil and cook in the preheated oven at 400°F (200°C) Gas 6 for 20 minutes.

Meanwhile, to make the topping, put the lemon zest into a bowl with the crushed garlic and mix well. Stir in the bread crumbs and cheese, then sprinkle over the top of the tian. Continue cooking for at least 30 minutes or until browned, finishing under the grill if necessary. Serve topped with basil leaves, if using.

These two vibrantly colored, hearty tagines are the perfect way to make entertaining easy. You can make the artichoke tagine with either fresh or frozen artichokes. If using fresh, you must first remove the outer leaves, then cut off the stems and scoop out the choke and hairy bits with a teaspoon. Place the artichokes in a bowl of cold water with lemon juice to prevent discoloration. The eggplant tagine is best made with baby vegetables, but you can also use slender, larger eggplants cut into quarters lengthwise.

tagine of artichokes, potatoes, peas, & saffron

2–3 tablespoons olive oil

2 red onions, halved lengthways, cut in half crossways, and sliced with the grain

4 garlic cloves, crushed

1 teaspoon cumin seeds

2 teaspoons coriander seeds

2 teaspoons ground turmeric

1–2 teaspoons dried mint

8 medium waxy potatoes, peeled and quartered

1½ cups/350 ml vegetable stock

4 prepared artichokes, quartered

a small bunch of fresh cilantro/coriander leaves, chopped

8 oz./225 g shelled fresh or frozen peas

½ preserved lemon, finely shredded

sea salt and freshly ground black pepper

a small bunch of fresh mint leaves, to serve

couscous or fresh, crusty bread, to serve

serves 4–6

Heat the olive oil in a tagine or heavy-based casserole dish, add the onion, and sauté until it begins to soften. Add the garlic, cumin and coriander seeds, ground turmeric, and the dried mint. Toss in the potatoes, coating them in the spices. Pour in the stock and bring it to a boil. Reduce the heat, cover with a lid, and cook gently for about 10 minutes.

Toss in the artichokes and fresh cilantro/coriander and cook for a further 5 minutes. Stir in the peas and preserved lemon, and season to taste with salt and pepper. Cook gently for 5–10 minutes, uncovered, until the artichokes are tender and the liquid has reduced.

Sprinkle with the fresh mint leaves and serve with couscous or chunks of fresh, crusty bread.

tagine of baby eggplants with cilantro & mint

1–2 tablespoons olive oil

1 tablespoon butter or ghee

1–2 red onions, halved lengthwise and sliced with the grain

3–4 garlic cloves, crushed

1–2 red chiles, seeded and sliced, or 2–3 dried red chiles, left whole

1–2 teaspoons cumin seeds, roasted and crushed

1–2 teaspoons coriander seeds, roasted and crushed

2 teaspoons sugar

16 baby eggplants/ aubergines, left whole with stalks intact

2 x 14-oz./400-g cans of chopped tomatoes

sea salt and freshly ground black pepper

a bunch of fresh mint leaves, roughly chopped

a bunch of fresh cilantro/coriander, roughly chopped

serves 4

Heat the oil and butter in a tagine or heavy-based casserole dish. Stir in the onions and garlic and sauté until they begin to color. Add the chiles, the cumin and coriander seeds, and the sugar. When the seeds give off a nutty aroma, toss in the baby eggplants/aubergines, coating them in the onion and spices. Add the tomatoes, cover with a lid, and cook gently for about 40 minutes, until the aubergines are beautifully tender.

Season to taste with salt and pepper and add half the mint and cilantro/coriander leaves. Cover and simmer for a further 5–10 minutes. Sprinkle with the remaining mint and cilantro/coriander leaves and serve hot.

This technique of cooking rice is Middle Eastern in origin, but has spread far and wide—similar rice dishes can be found in European, Latin American, Caribbean, Asian, and Indian cuisines, and it is known by many names including pilaf, pilau, and pulao. This version uses aromatic spices to flavor sweet orange vegetables. Delicious.

orange vegetable pilau

2 tablespoons light olive oil

1 onion, chopped

2 garlic cloves, chopped

1 tablespoon finely grated fresh ginger

1 large red chile, finely chopped

1 teaspoon ground coriander

1 teaspoon ground cumin

1 teaspoon turmeric

½ cup/50 g slivered/flaked almonds

1½ cups/300 g basmati rice

1 carrot, cut into large chunks

7 oz./200 g pumpkin or squash, peeled, seeded, and cut into wedges

1 small sweet potato, peeled and cut into thick half-circles

freshly squeezed juice of 1 lime

1 handful of fresh cilantro/coriander leaves, chopped

serves 4

Put the oil in a heavy-based saucepan and set over high heat. Add the onion, garlic, ginger, and chile and cook for 5 minutes, stirring often. Add the spices and almonds and cook for a further 5 minutes, until the spices become aromatic and look very dark.

Add the rice and cook for a minute, stirring well to coat the rice in the spices. Add the carrot, pumpkin, and sweet potato to the pan. Pour in 2½ cups/600 ml water and stir well, loosening any grains of rice that are stuck to the bottom of the pan. Bring to a boil, then reduce the heat to low, cover with a tight-fitting lid, and cook for 25 minutes, stirring occasionally.

Add the lime juice and cilantro/coriander, stir well to combine, and serve.

These two bakes are hearty, comforting, and tasty and are sure to delight guests, especially in the colder months. Bistro classic Macaroni Gratin is a much more sophisticated version of macaroni and cheese, and uses the superb Beaufort cheese (see note below). Fontina, used in the Mushroom, Spinach, & Potato Bake is a dense, nutty Italian cheese that melts beautifully and gives the mashed potatoes a wonderful golden crust.

macaroni gratin

10½ oz./300 g thin macaroni

2 cups/500 ml milk

3 tablespoons sour cream or crème fraîche

4 tablespoons/50 g unsalted butter

4 tablespoons all-purpose/plain flour

7 oz./200 g Beaufort cheese, finely grated*

coarse sea salt and freshly ground black pepper

a baking dish, 12 inch/ 30 cm long, greased with butter

serves 6

Cook the macaroni in plenty of boiling, well-salted water according to the instructions on the packet. Drain, rinse well, and return to the empty saucepan.

Heat the milk in a saucepan and stir in the sour cream. Melt the butter in a second saucepan over medium-high heat. Stir in the flour and cook, stirring constantly, for 3 minutes. Pour in the milk mixture and stir constantly until the mixture thickens. Season with salt and pepper.

Stir the milk mixture into the macaroni and taste, adding salt and pepper if necessary. Transfer to the baking dish and sprinkle with the cheese. Cook under a preheated broiler/grill until bubbling and browned, 10–15 minutes. Serve hot.

*Note Beaufort is an alpine cheese, similar to Gruyère, but with a slightly sweeter, more pronounced nutty flavor. It is becoming more widely available outside France, but if you cannot find it, Emmental, Cantal, or any firm, Cheddar-like cheese will do. The taste will be entirely different, of course.

mushroom, spinach, & potato bake

2¼ lb./1 kg floury potatoes

½ cup/125 ml whole milk

a pinch of freshly grated nutmeg

1 stick/125 g butter, cubed

1 lb./500 g small chestnut mushrooms, left whole and stalks removed

4 garlic cloves, roughly chopped

4 scallions/spring onions, cut into 1 inch/2.5 cm lengths

2¼ lb./1 kg fresh spinach, well washed and roughly chopped

7 oz./200 g fontina cheese, cubed

sea salt and freshly ground black pepper

a large, shallow baking dish

serves 4–6

Peel and roughly chop the potatoes. Put them in a large saucepan of lightly salted boiling water and boil for about 12–15 minutes, until tender but not falling apart. Drain well, return to the warm pan, and roughly mash. Add the milk and nutmeg and season to taste with salt and pepper. Beat with a wooden spoon or hand-held electric whisk until smooth. Stir through half of the butter, until well combined. Spoon about one-third of the mixture into the baking dish.

Preheat the oven to 350°F (180°C) Gas 4.

Heat half of the remaining butter in a large skillet set over medium heat. Add the mushrooms, garlic, and scallions/spring onions and gently fry for about 10 minutes, until golden. Spoon over the potato mixture in the baking dish.

Heat the remaining butter in the skillet and cook the spinach for 5 minutes, stirring often, until just wilted and tender. Season to taste and spoon over the mushrooms in the baking dish.

Spoon the remaining mashed potatoes on top of the spinach and scatter over the fontina. Bake in the preheated oven for about 30 minutes, until the cheese is bubbly and golden.

desserts

This is the most beautiful and delicious tart in the world. It tastes so delicate—and is lovely to serve to celebrate an occasion such as Valentine's Day or an anniversary.

rose petal tart

12 6z./350 g puff pastry, defrosted if frozen

rose-flavored filling
½ cup/150 ml plain or Greek yogurt
1 egg yolk
2–3 tablespoons rosewater
2 tablespoons superfine/caster sugar
1¼ cups/300 ml heavy/double cream

crystallized rose petals
1 egg white
petals of 2–4 scented roses
superfine sugar

a wire rack or baking parchment

a round or heart-shaped tart tin, 10 inch/25 cm diameter

foil and baking beans

makes one 10-inch/25-cm tart

To crystallize the rose petals, put the egg white into a bowl, beat until frothy, then paint onto clean, dry petals with a pastry brush. Sprinkle with superfine/caster sugar to coat completely, then arrange on a wire rack or baking parchment and leave in a warm place to dry out and crisp—at least overnight. Keep cool, but do NOT put into the refrigerator. Store between layers of kitchen paper in an airtight container.

Preheat the oven to 450°F (230°C) Gas 8.

Roll out the pastry as thinly as possible. Use to line the tart tin, pressing it into the sides and trimming to leave ¼ inch/½ cm hanging over the edge. Turn this inwards to make a rim. Prick the base all over with a fork, then chill or freeze for 15 minutes. Line with foil and baking beans, and bake blind for 12–15 minutes. Lower the oven temperature to 400°F (200°C) Gas 6, remove the foil and beans, and return to the oven for a further 5 minutes to dry out. You may have to flatten the pastry if it puffs up.

Turn the oven temperature down to 350°F (180°C) Gas 4. Put the yogurt, egg yolk, rosewater, and sugar into a bowl and mix well. Put the cream into a bowl and whisk until soft peaks form, then fold into the yogurt mixture. Spoon into the baked pastry shell, level the surface, and bake for about 20 minutes. The filling will seem almost runny, but will set as it cools. Cover and chill until firm.

Decorate with the crystallized rose petals. Serve slightly cold.

The term "cheesecake" is used loosely here as it has no biscuit base, but is a combination of a creamy ricotta base with a poached fruit topping. It is a wonderfully versatile dish as the rhubarb can be substituted for other seasonal fruits—it works a treat with poached pears in fall or winter.

poached rhubarb with pistachio & orange cheesecake

14 oz./400 g ricotta cheese

½ cup/60 g confectioners'/icing sugar

1 egg, lightly beaten

finely grated zest and freshly squeezed juice of 1 unwaxed orange

½ cup/70 g shelled unsalted pistachios

¼ cup/55 g granulated sugar

6 rhubarb stalks, cut into 1.5-inch/4-cm lengths

an 8 x 4-inch/20 x 10-cm loaf pan, lined with baking parchment

serves 4

Preheat the oven to 350°F (180°C) Gas 4.

Put the ricotta in a food processor with the confectioners'/icing sugar, egg, and orange zest and process until smooth. Stir the pistachios in, then spoon the mixture into the lined pan. Press down with the back of a large spoon, cover the pan with foil, and cook in the preheated oven for 50 minutes. Remove from the oven and let cool before removing from the pan.

Mix the orange juice, granulated sugar, and ½ cup/125 ml water in a small saucepan. Cook over high heat and boil for 5 minutes. Add the rhubarb and cook for 2–3 minutes over high heat, stirring often, until the rhubarb starts to soften. Transfer to a bowl and let cool to room temperature. Cut the baked ricotta into thick slices and serve with the poached fruit mixture spooned over the top.

Variation

Mix the rhubarb component of this recipe with some lightly whipped cream to make a simple fruit fool.

This is a classic French recipe for poached pears, but you can also poach them in a light syrup, then serve with a chocolate sauce and vanilla ice cream—also known as Poires Belle Hélène. For the meringue, don't use big figs, as they will split and prevent the egg whites cooking, making the meringue sloppy. If you can find them, small, very black ones are perfect with the caramelly meringue.

poached pears in honey wine

1 bottle of fruity red wine, 750 ml

4 tablespoons clear honey

a pinch of ground cinnamon

6 pears, ripe but not too soft

sweetened crème fraîche or whipped cream, to serve

serves 6

Put the wine, honey and cinnamon in a saucepan large enough to take all the pears snugly in one layer, stems upward. (Don't add the pears yet.) Bring to a boil, then simmer gently.

Using a vegetable peeler, peel the fruit, also leaving the stems intact. Put into the poaching liquid, stems upward. Poach until tender, 15–25 minutes depending on ripeness. Remove from the syrup with a slotted spoon. Raise the heat under the saucepan and boil the honey wine to reduce by half. Let cool.

Serve in small bowls, with some of the honey wine and a dollop of the cream of your choice.

fig & walnut meringue

1½ cups/150 g walnut halves

8–10 small black fresh figs, halved

6 large egg whites

1¼ cups/230 g soft light brown sugar

a 8-inch/20-cm diameter circle of baking parchment

serves 8–10

Preheat the oven to 350°F (180°C) Gas 4.

Put the walnuts on a baking sheet and toast in the preheated oven for 5 minutes, until just starting to turn golden. Remove and let cool. Leave the oven on.

Put the egg whites in a large, grease-free bowl and beat with an electric whisk until they form soft peaks. Add a tablespoon of the sugar at a time, beating well between each addition, and continue until all the sugar has been added and the meringue resembles a thick, fluffy caramel. Add the figs and walnuts and stir to combine.

Put the circle of baking parchment on a baking sheet. Use a large spoon to transfer the mixture onto the paper, keeping within the circle and using the back of the spoon to create dents and peaks for a rustic effect. Bake in the preheated oven for 40–45 minutes, until the peaks of the meringue are a dark golden color.

Let cool for 15 minutes then slide a large knife under the meringue to remove it from the paper and transfer it to a serving plate. This is best eaten warm or at room temperature.

Fresh berries are so tasty just as they are that it's tempting not to fuss with them too much. These gorgeous, sweet cheesecake pots are really simple, and you can also vary the idea with other fruits and curds (see Variation). Berries are also great used in a crumble—the tastiest of baked desserts. The floral aroma of blackberries can be enhanced by adding a small splash of Middle Eastern rosewater or orange blossom essence to the berries

lemon & blueberry upside-down cheesecakes

4 oz./115 g graham crackers or digestive biscuits

4 tablespoons/50 g butter

1 teaspoon ground cinnamon

9 oz./250 g mascarpone cheese

3–4 tablespoons homemade or storebought lemon curd

2–3 tablespoons low-fat/semi-skimmed milk

2–3 teaspoons freshly squeezed lemon juice, strained

9 oz./250 g fresh or frozen blueberries

a baking pan

4–6 small tumblers

serves 4–6

Preheat the oven to 375°F (190°C) Gas 5.

Put the graham crackers/biscuits in a plastic bag and crush with a rolling pin until you have even-size crumbs. (You can do this in a food processor but it tends to make them a bit fine and powdery.) Melt the butter in a small saucepan, stir in the cinnamon, cook for a few seconds, then stir in the crumbs until they have absorbed all the butter. Tip into the baking pan and bake in the preheated oven for 5 minutes until the crumbs are crisp. Set aside to cool.

Tip the mascarpone into a bowl and mix in the lemon curd with a wooden spoon until smooth. (Don't use an electric mixer—it will make the mixture seize up and become too buttery.) Add the milk to give a softer, more spoonable consistency and a little lemon juice to adjust the sweetness.

Divide the blueberries between the tumblers. Spoon over the mascarpone mixture and top with the crumbs. Cover the glasses with plastic wrap/clingfilm and refrigerate for an hour or so. (The bases can be made further in advance but don't add the crumble topping too far ahead otherwise it will go soggy.)

Variation

Try a delicious raspberry curd and mascarpone mix with fresh raspberries underneath; or a lime curd and kiwi fruit combination.

blackberry crumble

13 oz./375 g blackberries (about 2 baskets/punnets)

1 tablespoon granulated sugar

1 teaspoon cornstarch/cornflour

1 cup/130 g all-purpose/ plain flour

5 tablespoons/75 g unsalted butter, cubed and chilled

¼ cup/60 g light brown sugar

heavy/double cream, to serve

a medium ovenproof dish, lightly buttered

serves 4

Preheat the oven to 350°F (180°C) Gas 4.

Put the blackberries in a bowl with the granulated sugar and the cornstarch/cornflour and toss to mix. Tumble the berries into the buttered baking dish and set aside for 15–20 minutes.

Put the all-purpose/plain flour and butter in a large bowl and, using the tips of your fingers, rub the butter into the flour until the mixture resembles coarse breadcrumbs. Stir in the brown sugar.

Sprinkle the mixture evenly over the berries and bake in the preheated oven for 45–50 minutes, until the top is golden brown.

Let the crumble cool slightly before serving with dollops of cream spooned on top.

This sophisticated dessert is a combination of wonderful flavors—rich dark chocolate, fragrant cardamom, and roasted hazelnuts make it truly decadent. Try it served with a glass of Frangelico (hazelnut liqueur).

hazelnut, chocolate, & cardamom cream pie

pastry

5 tablespoons/60 g unsalted butter, softened

3 tablespoons/25 g confectioners'/icing sugar

1 cup/100 g hazelnuts

1 cup/125 g all-purpose/plain flour, unsifted

1 egg yolk

filling

10 green cardamoms

1¼ cups/300 ml heavy/double cream

7 oz./200 g good-quality dark chocolate (minimum 70% cocoa solids), broken into chunks

2 tablespoons/25 g unsalted butter

1 tablespoon cocoa powder, sifted, to decorate

a baking sheet

a 9-inch/23-cm fluted pie plate/flan tin

serves 8

Preheat the oven to 375°F (190°C) Gas 5.

Spread the hazelnuts out on a baking sheet and toast in the preheated oven for 15 minutes or until lightly browned. Cool, then chop in a food processor or coffee grinder (you may have to do this in batches). Cream the butter with the sifted confectioners'/icing sugar, add 1 tablespoon of the hazelnuts, then gradually work in the flour. Beat the egg yolk with 1 tablespoon water and add to the mixture, gradually pulling it into a ball.

Turn out onto a floured board or work surface and roll or press it out gently into a round slightly smaller than the pie plate/flan tin. Carefully lower it into the tin (don't worry if it breaks) and press it round and up the side until you have formed a pie crust/pastry case. Chill in the fridge for at least half an hour, then prick the base and bake it in the oven for about 15–20 minutes until lightly browned. Let cool.

Meanwhile, crush the cardamoms in a mortar with a pestle or with the end of a rolling pin. Remove the green husks and finely grind the seeds. Add to the cream and gently warm in a saucepan until the surface is just beginning to tremble. (Don't let it boil). Take off the heat and add the chocolate chunks, butter and the remaining ground hazelnuts. Set aside to cool, but don't let it get cold. Pour into the pie crust and put in the fridge for at least 2 hours. Dust the surface with cocoa powder before serving.

Here are two variations on classic, well-loved desserts. For the Tiramisù, soft amaretti are used instead of the traditional sponge fingers, as the distinctive taste of almond and kick of Kahlúa go wonderfully with the aromatic taste of coffee. This unusual way to make Chocolate Mousse uses confectioners' sugar, which makes it smoother, and crème fraîche for a pleasant tang.

rich almond tiramisù

10½ oz./300 g mascarpone cheese

3 tablespoons sugar

2 eggs, separated

10½–12 oz./300–350 g amaretti morbidi (soft amaretti)

½ cup/125 ml cold espresso

1½ tablespoons Kahlúa

cocoa powder and finely grated chocolate, to sprinkle

4 serving dishes, preferably glass

serves 4

Put the mascarpone, sugar, and egg yolks in a bowl and beat together until creamy.

In a clean, grease-free bowl, whisk the egg whites until they form stiff peaks. Fold a couple of spoonfuls of the egg whites into the mascarpone mixture, then fold in the remaining egg whites, one-third at a time.

Put a couple of spoonfuls of the mascarpone mixture into the base of four serving dishes and smooth the surface. Working carefully, soak about half the amaretti in the coffee for a minute or two until saturated (but not collapsing). Put a couple on top of the mascarpone, then sprinkle a little Kahlúa over each serving.

Continue layering with more mascarpone, coffee-soaked amaretti, and Kahlúa, and finish off with a layer of mascarpone. Dust with cocoa powder, then cover and chill overnight. To serve, sprinkle with cocoa powder and grated chocolate.

chocolate mousse

5½ oz./150 g dark chocolate, at least 70 per cent cocoa solids, finely chopped

4 tablespoons/50 g unsalted butter

5 large eggs, separated

⅓ cup/50 g confectioner's/icing sugar

¼ cup/50 g superfine/caster sugar

6 tablespoons crème fraîche or heavy/double cream

serves 6

Put the chocolate in a microwave-proof bowl and microwave on high for 40 seconds. Remove, stir and repeat until almost completely melted. Remove and stir in the butter. Set aside.

Put the egg whites and the confectioners'/icing sugar in another bowl and beat until they hold firm peaks. Set aside.

Put the egg yolks and sugar in a third bowl and beat until slightly thickened and a paler yellow. Using a spatula, fold in the cream. Stir in the chocolate mixture.

Add one-third of the beaten whites and mix until no streaks of white remain. Gently fold in the remaining whites, blending well but taking care not to overmix or you will deflate all the whites.

Transfer to individual serving dishes and refrigerate for 6–8 hours, or overnight. Serve chilled.

Note If you don't have a microwave, put the chocolate in a heatproof bowl over a saucepan of simmering water—don't let the water touch the bottom of the bowl. Leave until melted, stirring occasionally.

baking

Real sourdough takes several days of commitment; as in the method below, you make a starter from flour and water and leave it until it begins to ferment and give off a tangy, alcoholic aroma. However, from here, you have to feed the starter to encourage the yeast to multiply. This recipe skips this stage, just adding the starter to the bread dough so that you get the tangy flavor without the wait.

easy sourdough bread

3¼ cups/400 g rye flour

2 teaspoons sea salt

1⅔ cups/400 ml hand-hot water

¾ oz./20 g fresh yeast or
1 tablespoon/10 g easy-blend dried yeast/active dry yeast

2 cups/250 g whole-wheat/strong wholemeal bread flour

2 cups/250 g bread flour/strong white plain flour, plus extra for dusting

oil, for greasing

2 baking sheets, dusted with flour

makes 2 x 1-lb./450-g loaves

To make the starter, put 1¼ cups/150 g of the rye flour, the salt, and half of the hand-hot water in a large bowl. Cover with plastic wrap/clingfilm and leave at room temperature for 36 hours, by which time it should smell slightly tangy.

When you are ready to start making the dough, blend the yeast with the remaining hand-hot water (crumble it in if it is fresh yeast or sprinkle if it is dried). Transfer the remaining rye flour, and the whole-wheat/wholemeal and bread/white flours to a food mixer with a dough hook attachment. Alternatively, do this by hand. Set the mixer to the lowest speed and stir in the yeast mixture, followed by the sourdough starter, adding a little more warm water if it is still dry, to achieve a soft, slightly sticky dough.

Turn the mixer up (or use some elbow grease!) and knead the dough for 10–15 minutes. Place in a clean, lightly oiled bowl, cover with plastic wrap/clingfilm, and leave in a warm place for 1–2 hours, until it has almost doubled in size.

Gently push the air out of the dough and take it out of the bowl, keeping the top as untouched as possible as this will be the structure of your crust. Slice the dough in half and smooth the edges of each loaf by drawing the rough edges underneath and pinching them together on the underside. The tops should be smooth and slightly stretched, and the loaves round. Transfer to the prepared baking sheets, cover with a tea towel, and prove for 1 hour, until doubled in size. Meanwhile, preheat the oven to 450°F (230°C) Gas 8.

Dust the bread generously with flour and score the top with a criss-cross pattern. Sprinkle the sides of the oven with a little water. Bake the bread in the preheated oven for 5 minutes, then reduce the heat to 400°F (200°C) Gas 6 and bake for a further 25–30 minutes, until golden brown and hollow-sounding when tapped underneath. Leave to cool on a wire rack.

These two flavored breads make an exciting change from the norm. Cornbread is not really a bread at all but a crumbly, buttery cake. The soda bread is studded with raisins and streaked with lemon zest, making it even more delicious than plain soda bread. Slather them with butter and enjoy them for breakfast, served with strong black coffee.

chile & cheddar cornbread

1¼ cups/150 g all-purpose/plain flour

2 teaspoons baking soda/bicarbonate of soda

1 teaspoon sea salt

1 cup/150 g medium cornmeal or polenta

2 tablespoons sugar

5½ oz./150 g Cheddar cheese, grated

2 jalapeño chiles, chopped

1¼ cups/275 ml buttermilk

4 tablespoons/50 g butter, melted

1 egg, beaten

a 9-inch/22-cm round or 8-inch/20-cm square cake pan, greased

serves 6–8

Preheat the oven to 375°F (190°C) Gas 5.

Sift the flour and baking soda/bicarbonate of soda into a mixing bowl and stir in the salt, cornmeal, sugar, Cheddar cheese, and chiles.

In another bowl, beat together the buttermilk, butter, and egg. Pour into the dry ingredients and briefly fold in until no floury pockets remain. Scrape into the prepared cake pan and bake in the preheated oven for 20–25 minutes, until a skewer inserted into the centre comes out clean. Leave to cool in the tin for 5 minutes, then turn out onto a wire rack to cool completely.

lemon & raisin soda bread

1 cup/150 g raisins

3½ cups/400 g whole-wheat/wholemeal flour, plus extra for dusting

2 teaspoons baking soda/bicarbonate of soda

2 tablespoons sugar

1 teaspoon sea salt

1 cup/250 ml buttermilk

finely grated zest of 1 unwaxed lemon

a baking sheet, lightly floured

a 9-inch/22-cm round cake pan

serves 6–8

Preheat the oven to 425°F (220°C) Gas 7.

Soak the raisins in ¾ cup/200 ml water for 15 minutes.

Put the flour, baking soda/bicarbonate of soda, sugar, and salt in a large mixing bowl. Make a well in the centre and pour in the buttermilk, zest, raisins and their water, gradually drawing in the floury mixture with a wooden spoon until you have a soft, slightly loose but not sticky dough.

Bring the dough together with your hands and shape into a round roughly 9 inch/22 cm across and 2 inch/ 5 cm deep. Don't knead the dough or overwork it as you would with a yeasted bread—use a light touch as you would when making scones.

Place on the prepared baking sheet and score a large cross across the surface of the bread with a sharp knife. Dust with flour. Place the cake pan, upturned, on top of the bread to prevent it from browning too much. Bake in the preheated oven for 15 minutes. Reduce the heat to 400°F (200°C) Gas 6, remove the cake pan from on top of the bread and bake for a further 10–15 minutes, until it is hollow-sounding when tapped underneath. Leave to cool on a wire rack.

These look like the muffins which are sold in cafés and which seem to have exploded out of their pans with their generous proportions. There is no secret trick to this—just fill the muffin cases right up to the top!

exploding berry crumble muffins

3 cups/375 g all-purpose/plain flour

1 tablespoon baking powder

1 teaspoon baking soda/bicarbonate of soda

¾ cup/150 g granulated sugar

½ teaspoon salt

2 eggs, beaten

1 stick/115 g unsalted butter, melted

¾ cup/200 g sour cream

¼ cup/60 ml whole milk

6 oz./180 g raspberries

topping

¾ cup/100 g all-purpose/plain flour

5 tablespoons/75 g butter, chilled and cubed

2 tablespoons/30 g sugar

⅓ cup/30 g slivered/flaked almonds

a 12-hole muffin pan, lined with 12 paper cases

makes 12

Preheat the oven to 325°F (170°C) Gas 3. Line the muffin pan with paper cases and grease the surface of the pan where the muffins will rise and stick.

To make the topping, put the flour and butter in a food processor and pulse briefly, just until the butter is blended. Tip out into a bowl and add the sugar and almonds, pressing the mixture together with your hands.

To make the muffins, sift the flour, baking powder, baking soda/bicarbonate of soda, sugar and salt into a large mixing bowl. Put the eggs in a small pitcher/jug, add the melted butter, sour cream, and milk and whisk to combine. Pour the wet ingredients into the dry ingredients and scatter the raspberries on top. Using a large spoon, fold until the mixture is moistened. It needs to be lumpy and shouldn't be overworked otherwise the baked muffins will be tough.

Spoon the mixture into the paper cases right to the top. For regular-sized (not exploding!) muffins you can spoon the cases two-thirds full—you will be able to make more of these with this amount of mixture. Finish by scattering over the topping. Bake in the preheated oven for 25–28 minutes for large muffins, or 18–22 minutes for the smaller ones.

Leave the muffins to cool in the pan for 5 minutes before transferring to a wire rack.

These delicious teatime treats are sure to delight visiting family and friends. Studded with sweet glacé cherries and with a surprise layer of sticky marzipan running through the centre, this simple loaf cake will hit the spot. Or these buttery, melt-in-the-mouth cookies with a spicy ginger kick are perfect with a pot of warming lapsang souchong tea.

sticky marzipan & cherry loaf

1½ sticks/175 g butter, at room temperature

¾ cup/175 g granulated sugar

3 eggs

1¼ cups/175 g self-rising flour

3 oz./85 g ground almonds

6 oz./175 g candied/glacé cherries, halved

2¾ oz./75 g chilled marzipan, finely grated

confectioners'/icing sugar, for dusting

a 2-lb/900-g loaf pan, greased and lined

serves 8–12

Preheat the oven to 350°F (180°C) Gas 4.

Put the butter and sugar in a large bowl and beat until pale and creamy. Beat in the eggs, one at a time. Sift in the flour and fold in, then stir in the almonds and cherries until evenly distributed in the mixture.

Spoon half the mixture into the prepared loaf pan and level the surface. Sprinkle with the grated marzipan. Top with the remaining mixture and smooth the surface.

Bake for about 45 minutes, then remove the cake from the oven and cover the top with foil. Return it to the oven and bake for a further 25 minutes, until risen and golden and a skewer inserted in the centre of the cake comes out clean. Leave the cake to cool in the pan for about 10 minutes, then lift out on to a wire rack to cool. Serve the cake slightly warm or at room temperature.

stem ginger cookies

6 tablespoons/85 g butter, at room temperature

⅓ cup/75 g sugar

1 egg yolk

½ teaspoon ground ginger

2¼ oz./60 g stem ginger in syrup (about 3 balls), chopped

1 oz./25 g ground almonds

1 cup/115 g self-rising flour

2 baking sheets, lined with baking parchment

makes about 10

Preheat the oven to 325°F (160°C) Gas 3.

Beat the butter and sugar together until pale and creamy, then beat in the egg yolk. Stir in the ground ginger and stem ginger, then the ground almonds. Add the flour and mix well.

Roll the mixture into about ten walnut-sized balls and arrange them on the prepared baking sheets, spacing well apart. Flatten slightly with your fingers and bake for about 20 minutes, until a pale golden brown color.

Leave the cookies to cool on the baking trays for a few minutes, until slightly firm, then use a spatula to transfer them to a wire rack to cool.

These two cupcake recipes are perfect for newlyweds! Bake a batch of the delightfully flirtatious Love-heart Cupcakes and they'll never have eyes for anyone but you! Or try Warm Chocolate Muffins, eaten straight out of the oven whilst the chocolate is still soft and melting — irresistable. You could make them using milk instead of sour cream, but the sponge won't be as soft and crumbly.

raspberry love-heart cupcakes

1 stick/115 g butter, at room temperature

½ cup/115 g sugar

2 eggs

1 cup/115 g self-rising flour

grated zest and freshly squeezed juice of ½ lemon

to decorate

⅓ cup/80 ml sour cream or crème fraîche

1 tablespoon good-quality lemon curd

2¼ oz./60 g fresh raspberries

confectioners'/icing sugar, for dusting

a 12-hole muffin pan, lined with 12 paper cases

makes 12

Preheat the oven to 350°F (180°C) Gas 4, then line the muffin pan with paper cases.

Beat the butter and sugar together in a bowl until pale and fluffy, then beat in the eggs, one at a time. Sift the flour into the mixture and fold in, then stir in the lemon zest and juice. Spoon the mixture into the paper cases and bake for about 18 minutes until risen and golden and a skewer inserted in the centre comes out clean. Transfer to a wire rack to cool.

To decorate, using a sharp, pointed knife, remove a deep round from the centre of each cake, about 1½ inch/3 cm diameter. Slice the pointed bit off each piece of cored-out cake so that you are left with a flat round. Using a mini heart-shaped cutter, cut the rounds into heart shapes.

Combine the sour cream or crème fraîche and lemon curd in a bowl, then fold in the raspberries. Spoon the mixture into the hollowed-out cakes, then top with the hearts. Dust with confectioners'/icing sugar.

warm chocolate muffins

2¼ cups/275 g all-purpose/plain flour

3 tablespoons/30 g unsweetened cocoa powder

½ teaspoon baking soda/bicarbonate of soda

2½ teaspoons baking powder

6½ oz./185 g dark chocolate (60–70% cocoa solids), very roughly chopped

3½ oz./100 g milk chocolate (over 32% cocoa solids), grated

2 large eggs, beaten

½ cup/100 g light brown/muscovado sugar

1¼ cups/300 ml sour cream

1 stick/100 g unsalted butter, melted

a 12-hole muffin pan, lined with 12 paper cases

makes 12

Preheat the oven to 400°F (200°C) Gas 6, then line the muffin pan with paper cases.

Sift the flour, cocoa, baking soda/bicarbonate of soda, and baking powder in a large bowl and stir in the chopped and grated chocolates.

In a separate bowl, beat together the eggs, sugar, sour cream, and melted butter. Add the liquid mixture to the dry ingredients and stir until just combined and the mixture is fairly stiff. Don't over-mix otherwise the muffins will be tough. Spoon the mixture into the muffin pan holes to fill almost to the tops.

Bake for 20 minutes until risen and firm. Leave in the pan for about 15 minutes before turning out as the mixture is quite delicate: cakes made with sour cream or buttermilk have a lovely tender crumb. Turn carefully out onto a wire rack and serve warm or cool.

For a special occasion, this is a pretty and truly scrumptious cake that benefits from using the best white chocolate you can find. Check on the wrapper that it contains only cocoa butter, sugar, and milk solids and no other fat—this way you will get the best flavor. If you are pushed for time, dry the rose petals out in an oven set to the very lowest setting and leave the oven door ajar.

white chocolate mascarpone cake

3½ oz./100 g white chocolate (over 25% cocoa butter)

1½ sticks/175 g unsalted butter, softened

1 cup/200 g sugar

3 large eggs, separated, at room temperature

1 teaspoon vanilla extract

2 cups/250 g self-rising flour

⅓ cup/100 ml buttermilk or sour cream

3–4 tablespoons raspberry liqueur or raspberry vodka (optional)

crystallized rose petals

1 egg white

petals of 2 white or cream roses

superfine/caster sugar, to sprinkle

creamy white chocolate icing

6 oz./175 g white chocolate (over 25% cocoa butter)

12 oz./350 g mascarpone or soft cream cheese (such as Philadelphia), at room temperature

4 tablespoons/50 g unsalted butter, at room temperature

1 teaspoon vanilla extract

2 cups/300 g confectioners'/icing sugar, sifted

a pastry brush

a 9-inch/23-cm springform cake pan

serves 8

To crystallize the rose petals, beat the egg white until loosely frothy, then paint onto the rose petals with a pastry brush. Sprinkle with sugar to coat completely, arrange on a wire rack or non-stick baking parchment and leave in a warm place to dry out and crisp—at least overnight. Leave to cool, then store between layers of kitchen paper in an airtight container.

Preheat the oven to 350°F (180°C) Gas 4. Grease the bottom and sides of the cake pan and base and line with non-stick baking parchment. Dust the sides with flour and tap out the excess.

To make the cake batter, melt the chocolate with 6 tablespoons of water in a heatproof bowl over a pan of simmering water. Using an electric whisk, cream the butter, and sugar in a large bowl for about 5 minutes until pale and fluffy. Gradually beat in the egg yolks, one at a time, then beat in the melted white chocolate and the vanilla extract. Using a large metal spoon, fold in half of the flour, then the buttermilk, and then the remaining flour. Using a clean electric whisk, whisk the egg whites in a clean, dry bowl until just stiff but not dry. Beat one-third of the beaten egg whites into the cake mixture to loosen it, then carefully fold in the rest.

Spoon the batter into the prepared cake pan. Bake for 35 minutes, or until the cake springs back when touched in the centre and a fine skewer inserted in the centre comes out clean. Remove from the oven and leave to cool for 10 minutes in the pan, then turn out onto a wire rack, peel off the lining paper and leave to cool completely.

To make the creamy white chocolate icing, melt the chocolate (as above) and leave until almost cold. With an electric mixer, beat in the mascarpone, butter, and vanilla extract until smooth. Beat in the icing sugar until creamy and spreadable—you may not need it all. Cover and keep at room temperature.

Place the cake on a serving platter and prick all over with a skewer. Spoon over the raspberry liqueur and leave it to soak in for 30 minutes. Spread the icing all over the cake. Refrigerate until needed and scatter with the rose petals just before serving.

drinks

Smoothies are a winner for breakfast or a healthy snack. They are so quick to prepare and are a delicious way of increasing your intake of fruit—and all the vitamins, minerals and immune-boosting antioxidants that fruit contains.

banana magic

10½ oz./300 g fresh or frozen mixed berries, for example strawberries, raspberries, blueberries
2 bananas, chopped
1¼ cups/300 ml low-fat strawberry or raspberry yogurt
1 cup/250 ml unsweetened apple or orange juice (optional)
2 teaspoons clear honey (optional)

serves 2

Put the berries, banana, and yogurt in a blender. If using frozen fruits, add the unsweetened apple or orange juice. Blend until smooth. Add honey, to taste. Pour into glasses and serve.

tropical treat

1 ripe mango, peeled and chopped
2 bananas, chopped
¾ cup/200 ml freshly squeezed orange juice
2 passion fruits, halved

serves 2

Put the mango, banana, and orange juice in a blender and blend until smooth. Add the passion fruit pulp and seeds and stir. If the smoothie is too thick, add some extra orange juice to thin. Pour into glasses and serve.

blueberry blast

5½ oz./150 g blueberries
2 small bananas, chopped
1¼ cups/300 ml unsweetened apple juice

serves 2

Put the blueberries, banana, and apple juice in a blender and blend until smooth. Pour into glasses and serve.

Here are three fabulous cocktails for a special occasion or perhaps just after a long day! The James Bondi is an Australian variation on the classic Champagne cocktail. Campari and grapefruit juice are a marriage made in heaven, lovely with or without sugar. And the Peach Sangria is a white wine variation of the more classic Spanish aperitif, cool and delightful on a summer's day.

peach sangria

1 bottle chilled dry white wine
4 tablespoons peach liqueur
4 large ripe peaches, sliced
1 orange, sliced
1 unwaxed lemon, sliced
ice cubes
chilled lemonade

serves 6

Pour the wine into a large pitcher/jug, add the peach liqueur, sliced peaches, orange, and lemon. Add ice cubes and stir well. When ready to serve, half-fill tall glasses with the ice cubes, wine, and fruit, then top up with the lemonade.

Campari grapefruit slush

2¾ cups/600 ml ice cubes
½ cup/100 ml Campari
¾ cup/200 ml sweetened ruby grapefruit juice
sugar, to taste (optional)

serves 4

Put the ice cubes into a blender and grind until crushed. Add the Campari and grapefruit juice and blend until slushy. Add sugar to taste. Serve in chilled glasses with short cocktail straws.

James Bondi

6 brown sugar lumps
¼ cup/60 ml vodka
a dash of Angostura bitters
1 bottle chilled Champagne

serves 6

Put the sugar lumps into 6 Champagne flutes, add the vodka and stir with a spoon until the sugar completely dissolves (crush it slightly if necessary).

Add a dash of bitters to each one, top up with Champagne, and serve.

These two cocktails are a must for chocoholics. If you are feeling really devilish, you could float some more chocolate liqueur on top of the Chocotini.

chocotini

cocoa powder, to dip
2 parts vodka
1 part dark Crème de Cacao or other chocolate liqueur

a martini glass, chilled

a cocktail shaker

serves 1

Put some cocoa on a plate, wet the rim of the martini glass and dip it in the cocoa.

Fill the cocktail shaker with ice and pour over the vodka. Put on the top and shake really well for 1 minute. Remove the top and strain into the glass. Now slowly pour the Crème de Cacao into the glass, being careful not to touch the rim. The chocolate liqueur will sink to the bottom making a two-tone layered cocktail. Serve immediately and sip slowly.

le chocolatier

1 part Mozart Black Chocolate Liqueur or dark Crème de Cacao
1 part white rum
5½ oz./150 g good-quality dark chocolate ice cream
1 tablespoon grated dark chocolate

a tall glass, chilled

serves 1

Put the chocolate liqueur, white rum and ice cream in a blender. Process at low speed until evenly blended and pourable. Pour into the chilled glass and sprinkle with the grated chocolate. Serve immediately.

recipe basics

These two recipes are the foundation for so many dishes, they are very useful to have in your reportoire. Extracting the maximum flavor from vegetable stock is vital. The addition of the lentils adds an earthy flavor; brown rice can be used as an alternative. Béchamel is a classic white roux sauce that forms the basis of dishes such as lasagne, but is rarely served as a sauce in itself.

vegetable stock

2 tablespoons extra virgin olive oil

2 garlic cloves, peeled

1 onion, roughly chopped

1 large leek (outer layer removed and reserved for the bouquet garni) and chopped

2 carrots, chopped

2 potatoes, cubed

2 celery ribs/sticks, chopped

⅔ cup/150 ml dry white wine

1 ripe tomato, chopped

4½ oz./125 g mushrooms, chopped

⅓ cup/50 g red lentils

2 teaspoons sea salt

bouquet garni

outer layer from a 3-inch/8-cm length of leek

a 3-inch/8-cm length of celery rib

1 garlic clove, peeled

2 fresh bay leaves (or 1 dried)

2 fresh flat leaf parsley sprigs

2 fresh thyme sprigs

6 black peppercorns

makes approximately 7 cups/1.75 litres

To make the bouquet garni for the stock, open the outer layer of leek out flat. Put the remaining ingredients on top of the leek skin, then roll up tightly. Tie up with kitchen twine.

Heat the olive oil in a large saucepan and fry the garlic, onion and leek for 10 minutes. Add the carrots, potatoes, and celery and fry for a further 10 minutes, or until softened but not colored.

Add the wine and boil rapidly for 2–3 minutes, or until almost completely reduced. Add the remaining ingredients, the bouquet garni, and 7 cups/1.75 litres cold water and bring to a boil. Cover and simmer for 1 hour.

Strain the stock through a fine strainer/sieve and leave to cool completely. Refrigerate for up to 3 days.

béchamel sauce

2 onions, roughly chopped

4 fresh bay leaves

4 whole cloves

5 cups/1.2 litres milk

6 tablespoons/80 g unsalted butter

⅔ cup/80 g all-purpose/plain flour

sea salt and freshly ground black pepper

makes approximately 5 cups/1.2 litres

Put the onions, bay leaves, cloves, milk, and seasoning into a saucepan, bring to a boil and immediately remove from the heat. Set aside to infuse for about 20 minutes, then strain.

To make the roux, melt the butter in a clean saucepan, add the flour, and cook over medium heat, stirring, for 1 minute. Gradually stir in the strained milk and continue to cook, stirring, until the mixture boils. Simmer for 2 minutes and remove from the heat.

Variation

Mornay Sauce

1 quantity Béchamel Sauce (see above)

7 oz./200 g grated Cheddar or other cheese

Heat the béchamel sauce and stir in the Cheddar until melted. Serve hot.

This collection of recipes is indispensible for adding flavor to all sorts of dishes, from salads and grilled vegetables, to pastas and breads. Be sure to use very good olive oil for the aïoli and pesto; the flavor base comes from the oil, so it is worth investing in something special.

aïoli

2 egg yolks
1⅔ cups/400 ml best-quality extra virgin olive oil
6 large garlic cloves
fine sea salt

makes approximately 1⅔ cups/400 ml

Put the egg yolks in a small, deep bowl. Whisk well, then gradually whisk in the oil, adding it bit by bit and whisking vigorously, until the mixture is as thick as mayonnaise. Stir in the garlic and season to taste.

balsamic glaze

a 16-oz./500-ml bottle balsamic vinegar

makes approximately ½ cup/125 ml

Pour the vinegar into a small saucepan and boil gently until it is reduced by about two-thirds and reaches the consistency of a thick syrup. Pour straight into a sterilized bottle or jar and leave to cool. Seal and store in a cool place.

pesto genovese

2 garlic cloves
½ cup/50 g pine nuts
2 big handfuls fresh basil leaves
⅔ cup/150 ml extra virgin olive oil, plus extra to preserve
4 tablespoons/50 g unsalted butter, softened
4 tablespoons freshly grated Parmesan cheese
sea salt and freshly ground black pepper

makes approximately 1 cup/250 ml

Peel the garlic and put it in a pestle and mortar with a little salt and the pine nuts. Pound until broken up. Add the basil leaves, a few at a time, pounding and mixing to a paste. Gradually beat in the olive oil, little by little, until the mixture is creamy and thick.

Alternatively, put everything in a food processor and process until just smooth.

Beat in the butter and season with pepper, then beat in the Parmesan. Spoon into a screw-top jar with a layer of olive oil on top to exclude the air, then store in the refridgerator, for up to 2 weeks, until needed.

Although making puff pastry can be daunting, this cheat's recipe is really easy —but the butter must be very hard as it is grated into the mixture. The pastry can be used for the tarts on pages 43, 62, 110, and 126, if you prefer to make your own.

cheat's rough puff pastry

2 cups/250 g all-purpose/plain flour
a pinch of salt
1½ sticks/150 g unsalted butter, frozen
about ½ cup/150 ml iced water

makes about 1 lb/500 g pastry, enough to line a tart tin 12 inches/30 cm diameter

Sift the flour and salt into a large bowl. Hold the butter in a tea towel and, using the large side of a box grater, quickly grate the butter into the flour. (see picture A). Stir the butter into the flour with a round-bladed knife until evenly distributed. Sprinkle the water over the surface, then mix with the knife until the dough starts to come together in a messy lump (see picture B).

Tip the mixture onto a floured work surface and knead lightly until it forms a streaky, rather lumpy ball. Flatten the ball with the palm of your hand. Wrap in plastic wrap/clingfilm and chill for 30 minutes until firm.

Unwrap the dough and roll out away from you into a rectangle 3 times longer than it is wide—no exact measurements are needed here, but it should be about ½ inch/1 cm thick (see picture C). Remove any excess flour with a pastry brush.

Lightly mark the pastry into 3 equal sections with a blunt knife. Fold the third closest to you up over the middle third, then bring the top third towards you over the folded two-thirds. Make a finger mark in the pastry to indicate you have completed 1 roll, then fold (see picture D). Rewrap and chill for 15 minutes.

Repeat twice more (indenting each time with the number of roll and folds completed). Wrap and chill for 30 minutes. Roll to the shape, then chill for 30 minutes.

Pizza is an amazingly versatile dish that can be adapted to whatever you have in the store cupboard. This dough recipe will make the typical Neapolitan pizza—soft and chewy with a crisp crust or cornicione. Pizzaiola sauce is a speciality of Naples, but is quite common throughout Italy. To acquire its concentrated, almost caramelized flavor, the tomatoes must be fried over a lively heat.

basic pizza dough

1 cake/25 g fresh yeast, 1 packet easy blend dried dried yeast or 2 teaspoons quick-rising yeast

½ teaspoon sugar

1 cup/250 ml hand-hot water

4 cups/500 g unbleached white bread flour or Italian

"0" or "00" grade flour, plus extra to dust

1 teaspoon fine sea salt

1 tablespoon olive oil

makes 2 medium-crust pizzas, 10–12 inch/25–30 cm

In a medium bowl, cream the fresh yeast with the sugar and whisk in the hand-hot water. Leave for 10 minutes until frothy. For other yeasts, follow the packet instructions.

Sift the flour and salt into a large bowl and make a well in the centre. Pour in the yeast mixture, then the olive oil. Mix together with a round-bladed knife, then use your hands until the dough comes together. Tip out onto a lightly floured surface, then knead briskly for 5–10 minutes until smooth, shiny, and elastic. (5 minutes for warm hands, 10 minutes for cold hands!) Don't add extra flour at this stage—a wetter dough is better. If you feel the dough is sticky, flour your hands, not the dough. The dough should be quite soft. If it is really too soft, knead in a little more flour.

To test if the dough is ready, roll it into a fat sausage, take each end in either hand, lift the dough up, and stretch the dough outwards, gently wiggling it up and down—it should stretch out quite easily. If it doesn't, it needs more kneading. Shape the dough into a neat ball. Put in an oiled bowl, cover with a damp kitchen/tea towel, and leave to rise in a warm, draught-free place until doubled in size—about 1½ hours.

Uncover the dough, punch out the air, then tip out onto a lightly floured work surface. Divide into 2 and shape into smooth balls. Place the balls well apart on non-stick baking parchment, cover loosely with plastic wrap/clingfilm, and leave to rise for 60–90 minutes. Use as desired.

pizzaiola sauce

½ cup/125 ml olive oil

2 garlic cloves, chopped

1 teaspoon dried oregano

2 x 14-oz./400-g cans chopped tomatoes or 2 lb./800 g fresh tomatoes, halved and cored

sea salt and freshly ground black pepper

makes about 1⅔ cups/400 ml

In a large, shallow pan, heat the oil almost to smoking point (a wok is good for this).

Standing back to avoid the spluttering, add the garlic, oregano, and tomatoes. Cook over a fierce heat for 5–8 minutes or until the sauce is thick and glossy. Season.

Pass the sauce through a food mill (mouli) set over a bowl, to remove seeds and skin. You can put the smooth sauce back in the pan to reduce it further if you like.

Ladle the sauce into the centre of the pizza base and spread it out in a circular motion with the back of the ladle before topping with your preferred ingredients.

index

recipe credits

Ghillie Başan

spicy carrot & chickpea tagine with honey

tagine of artichokes, potatoes, peas, & saffron

tagine of baby eggplants with cilantro & mint

Fiona Beckett

feta, cucumber, & mint salad

hazelnut, chocolate, & cardamom cream pie

heirloom tomato, bell pepper, & mozzarella tart

lemon & blueberry upside-down cheesecakes

Susannah Blake

butternut squash & blue cheese giant toasts

raspberry love-heart cupcakes

rich almond tiramisù

stem ginger cookies

sticky marzipan & cherry loaf

Celia Brooks Brown

roasted teriyaki tofu steaks with glazed green vegetables

Maxine Clark

basic pizza dough

cheat's rough puff pastry

cherry tomato, bocconcini, & basil bruschetta

chocotini

gnocchi with arugula pesto

rose petal tart

le chocolatier

pear, pecorino, & pea crostini

pesto genovese

pizzaiola sauce

warm chocolate muffins

white chocolate mascarpone cake

Ross Dobson

asparagus, corn, & goat cheese frittata

asparagus & goat cheese tart

baked ricotta with roasted cherry tomato salsa

beet & caraway dip

blackberry crumble

caramelized onion palmiers

Champagne risotto with lemon thyme tomatoes

chile-roasted vegetables with soft goat cheese

corn relish

creamy vegetable & cashew curry

eggplant, tomato & red lentil curry

fig & walnut meringue

foraged mushroom risotto

lime pickle & vegetable biryani

miso & Parmesan palmiers

mozzarella, peach, & frisée salad

mushroom, spinach, & potato bake

naked spinach & ricotta ravioli with sage cream

Napolitana lentil stew

Niçoise-style brown rice salad with fresh herbs

orange vegetable pilau

paella of summer vine vegetables with almonds

pappardelle pasta with portobello mushrooms & chestnuts

pappardelle pasta with roast fennel, tomato, & olives

pickled eggplant

poached rhubarb with pistachio & orange cheesecake

pumpkin & Gorgonzola risotto

roasted parsnip & garlic dip

slow-roasted tomatoes

smoky hotpot of great northern beans

soft goat cheese & fennel tart

Spanish-style panzanella

spiced carrot dip

Taleggio & potato tortilla with red bell pepper tapenade

tempura of mixed veggies with citrus dipping sauce

tenderstem broccoli, shiitake, & tofu omelet

tomato & mozzarella salad with eggplant relish

truffled egg linguine

upside-down bell pepper & tomato pie

wild mushroom lasagne

Tonia George

blueberry pancakes

buckwheat & banana pancakes

chile & Cheddar cornbread

couscous with feta, dill, & spring beans

dairy-free coconut pancakes with lime syrup & mango

easy sourdough bread

exploding berry crumble muffins

French onion soup

hash browns

herb fritters with fried eggs & sumac tomatoes

lemon & raisin soda bread

orange cornmeal hotcakes with orange flower syrup

pink grapefruit with vanilla sugar

poached eggs on spinach with yogurt & spiced butter

stir-fried vegetables & tofu with lime leaves & honey

tagliatelle with peas & goat cheese pesto

tortilla with potatoes, chiles, & piquillo peppers

winter-spiced salad with pears, honeyed pecans, & ricotta

Rachael Anne Hill

banana magic

blueberry blast

cinnamon porridge

Florentine baked eggs

huevos rancheros

morning muffins

spiced pear, apricot, & fig compote

tropical treat

Caroline Marson

harissa-spiced chickpeas with halloumi & spinach

Moroccan-style roasted vegetable couscous

Jane Noraika

feta & chickpea parcels with onion and tomato chutney

Elsa Petersen-Schepelern

pumpkin soup

Louise Pickford

balsamic glaze

béchamel sauce

Campari grapefruit slush

James Bondi

peach sangria

quick vegetable curry

simple tomato & olive tart with Parmesan

vegetable stock

Fiona Smith

ratatouille

tomato, avocado, & lime salad with crisp tortillas

Sonia Stevenson

Provençal tian

Sunil Vijayakar

spiced potatoes

Laura Washburn

aïoli

chocolate mousse

creamy potato gratin

harissa potatoes

macaroni gratin

new potatoes baked with sea salt

poached pears in honey wine

photography credits

Martin Brigdale
Pages 2, 47, 79, 105, 112, 113,
118, 119, 122, 126, 127, 130,
136, 137, 139bg, 146–148,
161ac, 164, 167

Peter Cassidy
Pages 8, 17bg, 36, 39, 57al, 63,
68, 71, 75ar, 76, 89bg, 97, 100,
106, 108, 111, 117, 121, 135,
139ac, 144, 149, 150, 153al,
153ar, 153bg, 156, 158, 159

Lisa Cohen
Pages 12, 88, 170

Nicki Dowey
Pages 24, 27, 155

Tara Fisher
Page 154

Gus Filgate
Pages 40, 41

Jonathan Gregson
Pages 17al, 19–21, 26, 28,
30–32, 89ac, 138, 139al, 139ar,
140–142, 145, 152, 153ac

Winfried Heinze
Pages 10, 18

Richard Jung
Pages 6, 29, 34, 35ac, 35ar,
42–46, 49–51, 53, 57ar, 58–60,
65, 83, 85, 89al, 89ar, 90–92,
95, 96, 99, 101–104, 110, 114,
115, 120, 124, 125ar, 128, 129,
131–134, 143, 160, 161al, 162,
165, 166, 168, 169

Lisa Linder
Page 94

William Lingwood
Pages 25, 33, 70, 78, 93, 107,
109ac, 116

Diana Miller
Pages 48, 52, 62, 73, 87

David Munns
Pages 54, 55, 61

© Steve Painter
Page 35bg

Daniel Pangbourne
Page 57bg

William Reavell
Pages 17ar, 22, 23, 57ac, 64, 69,
72, 86

Yuki Sugiura
Page 37

Debi Treloar
Endpapers pages 1, 3, 9, 14, 16,
17ac, 35al, 74, 75al, 109bg,
125al, 125ac

Simon Upton
Page 84

Ian Wallace
Pages 161ar, 163

Kate Whitaker
Pages 4, 5, 7bg, 11, 13, 15bg,
38, 56, 66, 67, 75ac, 75bg, 77,
80–82, 98, 109al, 109ar, 123,
125bg, 161bg

Polly Wreford
Pages 7 inset, 15 inset, 151, 170

Francesca Yorke
Page 157